FORGIVING MOTHER

FORGIVING MOTHER

A Marian Novena of Healing and Peace

MARGE STEINHAGE FENELON

franciscan
media
Cincinnati, Ohio

Cover design by Candle Light Studios
Book design by Mark Sullivan

Library of Congress Cataloging-in-Publication Data
Names: Fenelon, Marge, author. Title: Forgiving mother : a novena of healing and peace / Marge Fenelon. Description: Cincinnati : Servant, 2017. | Includes bibliographical references. Identifiers: LCCN 2017040511 | ISBN 9781632532275 (trade paper) Subjects: LCSH: Motherhood—Religious aspects—Catholic Church. | Catholic women—Religious life. | Mary, Blessed Virgin, Saint. Classification: LCC BX2353 .F47 2017 | DDC 242/.6431—dc23 LC record available at https://lccn.loc.gov/2017040511

Published by Franciscan Media
28 W. Liberty St.
Cincinnati, OH 45202
www.FranciscanMedia.org

Printed in the United States of America.
Printed on acid-free paper.
19 20 21 5 4 3

❈⤜⟡⤛❈

To Pitter, Palaluchi, and Kleine Joey
from Maakie

Contents

• • •

Donna-Marie Cooper O'Boyle

Each one of us was blessed with a mother. We each have a unique story. What makes our stories different could be how we have been mothered. There is no perfect family. We must remember that we are always a work in progress, stumbling along the way that leads to heaven—our real home. But we need the help from a loving mother to find our way.

For some mothers, nurturing their children comes very naturally. Some might say that they were "born to be a mother." I felt that way raising my children. I fully embraced the miraculous vocation of motherhood, taking in every moment and feeling the need to fully nurture my children with unconditional love. That does not mean that it was always easy. Mothers all around the world are unappreciated, misunderstood, and bombarded with mixed messages from a convoluted culture dictating to them that they should perhaps be pursuing something else instead of an oftentimes thankless role. I tell about this in my many books on motherhood, and in my memoir *The Kiss of Jesus*, in which I share my crooked path through life—being held at gun point by a crazed man, being abandoned by my spouse on the side of the road, suddenly becoming a single mother when I was about to give birth to my third child, and some harrowing experiences too.

The children and I survived some turbulent times. Later on, more challenges would unfold to an even greater degree. Survival mode became my middle name, but I was so thoroughly immersed in God's amazing grace and Mother Mary's assistance. Along the way, I met St. Teresa of Calcutta, who became a spiritual mother to me—my other mother. I now do all I can to pass along the wisdom I learned from her. One such lesson she often preached was "Love begins at home." Something so simple yet profound. We must examine our priorities and be sure that we are loving those at home before setting out to save the world. We must not inadvertently neglect the very ones given to us by God to care for.

My own mother seemed to make everything better—throughout every joy and every struggle. She set a powerful prayer example in our humble domestic church. It is something that has stayed with me—deeply etched on my heart—carried into my own domestic church throughout thick and thin years. God was with us—every step of the way—and always will be.

At times, we fail to recognize our Lord and his holy mother in our lives because we may feel overwhelmed in dark and troubled times that we experience. We might not feel the love or nurturing from our own mothers, which can deeply affect us. Many of us are the walking wounded. Countless women feel unequipped to mother their children in the way they are called to do because they are lacking the essential mother's love so necessary for survival. Yes, I did say "survival."

Studies have proven the absolute need to love and nurture our children, or else they wither away, their growth stunted in many areas. They simply will not mature appropriately. Centuries ago, in a bizarre Prussian experiment, babies in an orphanage were not given the attention they needed between feedings. Tragically, they all died a senseless death. Similarly, all throughout the world, children not loved appropriately by their mothers, experience deep pain and many times long-lasting crippling wounds.

When I was on complete bed rest during a precarious pregnancy in which I had a heart condition and hemorrhaging uterus, my dear spiritual mother Mother Teresa sent me a blessed Miraculous Medal, which is a special medal of the Blessed Mother. Mother Teresa also told me to pray to the Blessed Mother and pray, "Mary, mother of Jesus, be mother to me now." The key words here are "mother" and "now." We need Mary *now*. I prayed that prayer often and now teach it to others. As I write this foreword, my daughter of that pregnancy, Mary-Catherine, is turning twenty-six years old. Today is her birthday! The main point of Mother Teresa's simple prayer is that we need to reach out to Jesus's mother, get to know her more intimately, and ask for her help. She is not some abstract or faraway saint. She is with us, even and especially now. She wants to mother us. After all, it was her son, Jesus, as he was dying on the cross who gave the eminent gift of his mother to us. He wants us to know her and to love her and to ask for her beautiful intercession. Jesus wants us to ask her to be our mother.

Mary is no stranger to the realities and hardships of life. We can recall that her son's lifeless body was placed into her arms when he was taken from the cross. She stood with him all the way to the cross and beyond. She knows suffering and intense pain. She will understand our hearts too.

Author Marge Fenelon so aptly explains the role of Mother Mary in our lives in *Forgiving Mother*. In the introduction, she writes:

> I want you to know and feel that you are a child of Mary and that she loves you tenderly. She really, truly is your mother— given to you by our Lord as he hung dying on the cross. Jesus

wants you to accept his mother as your own and to develop a deepening relationship with her so that she can fill the void that the past has left inside of you. And in her kind, motherly way, she will. What's more, she will lead you to her son who, as God, is the ultimate source of all healing and peace.

For those who struggle from a "mother wound," hope and healing are available through God's amazing grace and within a deepening and ongoing relationship with our Blessed Mother. Marge Fenelon points out that "with or without a professional, Mary, with her motherly love and intercessory power, is a vital element of deep and long-lasting healing." Further, the author states, "She will lead you to her merciful Son so that he can affect forgiveness, healing, and peace in you."

Yes, Mother Mary always leads us to her son, Jesus. When a bride and groom were without wine at the wedding feast at Cana, Mary said, "Do whatever He tells you." She is forever leading us to her son. Allow the author to take you by the hand through the pages of this book and lead you into something quite magnificent. I know that you will be glad that you did. I can guarantee it. I also believe that *Forgiving Mother* will edify any reader, helping them to understand the need to love and nurture one another as well as learn more about Mary's essential role in our lives.

In the words of my dear other mother, St. Teresa, "Mary, mother of Jesus, be mother to me now."

Some folks joke about having a double so that they can be two places at once and get more done.

Well, I actually have that, sort of.

What I mean is that there are two Marge Fenelons. More precisely, there are two Margaret Fenelons. As you can imagine, it confuses a whole lot of people. Because of that, and especially because of the sensitive nature of this book, my wonderful editor and I decided that it would be good to include an explanation of this unusual circumstance.

The explanation is easy; getting people to remember it is an awful lot harder. You see, both of us Margarets married into the Fenelon family. There's a funny story told in the family that my mother-in-law and father-in-law were positive that the last child to be born in the family was a girl. Believing that, my father-in-law decided he wanted their baby girl to be named Margaret. When my mom-in-law went into labor, she and my dad-in-law were eager to meet their little Margaret. Well, out popped—a boy! Instead of giving birth to their own Margaret, the Fenelons were later given two Margarets through the marriages of their sons!

The two of us Margarets do have a lot in common, particularly our ties to the Apostolic Movement of Schoenstatt and its founder, Fr. Joseph Kentenich.

While we have much in common, there are some vast differences that need to be known for readers of *Forgiving Mother*.

The other Marge Fenelon and I have completely different backgrounds. The other Marge was born into a solid, loving, devotedly Catholic family. Her parents were excellent examples of living the Catholic faith and sensible, nurturing parenting. They have both passed away, and I knew them personally before they died. They were amazing people, and I love them dearly.

Perhaps you see my dilemma. I am sure beyond doubt that I've been called by God to share with you my childhood in light of healing from the effects of an abusive mother and about the miracles Mary has done in my life and will do in yours. But I don't for a single second want anyone to confuse my parents with the parents of the other Marge Fenelon, particularly our two mothers—one mentally ill and abusive, the other kind and holy. Nor do I want anyone to confuse the two of us Marges, because I do not want any damage done to her or her parents' reputations. We are often confused as it is—something I find affectionately amusing—but now the distinction needs to be made concretely clear. I am very intent on that, out of love and respect for my sister-in-law.

You will know me by my maiden name. With my siblings' permission, I will share that with you. I am Marge (Margaret) Steinhage Fenelon, and I promise you that there are no Marge Fenelons with that same maiden name.

I hope this clears things up for you, because it is admittedly an unusual and confusing situation. More than anything else, I hope and pray that, by daring to share my story, I will be helping you to open up channels of forgiveness, healing, and peace for you as well as for your mom. May our Mother Mary bless, guide, and comfort you!

Introduction

What goes on inside of you when you hear the word *mother*? Perhaps it brings happy memories of the loving woman who tended you when you were younger and who continues to care for you now. Or maybe it brings about quite a different response. Could it be that the word *mother* elicits hurtful memories of discord, abuse, neglect, disharmony, or estrangement?

If so, then this book is written for you and the many others like you who struggle with painful memories and difficult relationships with their mothers.

For the most part, all mothers want to do the best for their children. Or, at least, they do the best they can with what they have been given—or have not been given, as the case may be. Oftentimes, they themselves have not experienced the love and nurturing of a capable and balanced mother. And so they suffer, and because of their suffering, their children suffer, too.

I know, because I am one of those children who has suffered with painful memories and a difficult relationship with my mother. I know the pain, fear, hopelessness, insecurity, resentment, and anger of being raised by a troubled mother. I also know the way out—Mary.

My mother was a tormented woman. Raised by an alcoholic father and gambling-addicted mother, the abuse she suffered scarred her for life. I believe she did the best she could with what she had. But her wounds were just too deep, too extensive. There are some wonderful things that she did, but for the most part, her wounds kept her from being the truly loving, noble wife and mother she could have been.

For that reason, I was always on guard and, at the urging of my spiritual advisor, had to distance myself from her as much as possible. Eventually, I had to separate myself from her completely in order to protect myself, but especially my children. It was painful, but necessary.

In spite of the difficulties, I was brought up in what I consider a fairly Catholic home, and my three siblings and I all received a Catholic education. When I look back, I can see that Mary had her hand on me from the start. I was a sickly child, and because of that, I spent a goodly amount of time lying on the couch in our living room. Right above the couch hung a beautiful portrait of Mary tenderly holding baby Jesus. Some of my earliest memories are of resting on the couch and looking up at that picture. It gave me great comfort.

When I went to grade school, I often became quite homesick—to the point of tears. One day as I was crying for home, the teacher, a Schoenstatt Sister of Mary, took me out of the classroom, down the hall, out the door, onto the playground and to a tiny white house on the playground. I am sure she did it to get me to stop crying and before I got the rest of the children crying along with me! When we reached the little white house, Sister opened the door, and there I saw a large copy of my picture of Mary hanging inside. As six-year-olds are prone to do, I assumed the whole world was about me. I was convinced that the sisters who taught in the school had hung that picture in the little house just so I would not be homesick anymore!

I soon learned that the picture had not been hung there just for me, as I had naively presumed. The little house was a Schoenstatt Marian Shrine, and the portrait both inside the shrine and in our living room was the *Mother Thrice Admirable, Queen and Victress of Schoenstatt*—patroness of the Apostolic Movement of Schoenstatt, a worldwide Catholic lay movement of renewal in Christ through Mary. As a young adult, I learned that Schoenstatt's founder and servant of God, Fr. Joseph Kentenich (1885–1968), had given the picture to my mother during a chance meeting when I was just a year old. At that meeting, Fr. Kentenich blessed me and consecrated me to the Blessed Virgin Mary. There is no doubt in my mind that this act of consecration to Mary is what has protected me all the days of my life since then! That experience planted the seed for me to one day forgive and grow from my painful past. In Mary, I discovered the mother I longed for and the mother I desperately needed.

I want that for you. I want you to know and feel that you are a child of Mary and that she loves you tenderly. She really, truly is your mother—given to you by our Lord as he hung dying on the cross. Jesus wants you to accept his mother as your own and to develop a deepening relationship with her so that she can fill the void that the past has left inside of you. And in her kind, motherly way, she will. What's more, she will lead you to her son, who, as God, is the ultimate source of all healing and peace.

Humans are spiritual beings, and for that reason, it is not enough to simply think things through. You cannot mentally power through healing; your spirit needs to be involved as well. That is why prayer is an essential part of the healing process. Through prayer, you will draw closer to Mary and her son so that they can guide you in letting go of the past and reaching toward healing and peace. Prayer will obtain for you the grace you need to be strong, courageous, patient, and faithful in the process of recovering from the suffering you have endured. Prayer will help you, little by little, to entrust yourself to Mary's motherly embrace and to completely surrender yourself—and your mother—to Jesus.

In Part One of *Forgiving Mother*, I have written about the process of moving from fear to forgiveness. I share with you some of my own experiences so that you can see that I really do understand what you are going through. It has been scary to make myself so vulnerable! Yet, I am convinced that writing this book is God's will, and I pray that it will do great good for many people. I also used wisdom from Church documents, Scripture, and the saints that will help you deal with the painful memories, emotions, and fears that are a result of your past. It's only in facing the past that we can confidently face the future.

Part Two of *Forgiving Mother* includes a novena (*novena* means "nine") for healing and peace. A novena is a series of nine consecutive prayers—usually one per day—for a particular intention. The days of this novena correspond to the book's nine primary chapters and are like stepping stones that lead you, prayerfully, through the journey from hurt to healing. Using inspiration, reflections, and resolutions, the novena will deepen your relationship with Mary as your Mother and call upon Christ to make you well. Pray through it, meditate on it, and let it sink into your heart and soul. Be gentle with yourself. Healing is a process, not a project, and you must, through prayer, allow God's grace to work in you. You may wish to pray one day of the novena after you read each primary chapter, or you may wait to pray it straight through at the end. Likely, you will feel the need to go through it again and again, as healing is more of a cyclical process than a linear one. Regardless, take your time and pray it in the way that is most beneficial for you. This is *your* healing process, and no one else's.

Of course, it is sometimes necessary to seek professional help, and there is absolutely no shame in that. In fact, you must do that if you sense the need, or you could endanger your well-being. With or without a professional, Mary, with her motherly love and intercessory power, is a vital element of deep and long-lasting healing. She will lead you to her merciful son so that he can affect forgiveness, healing, and peace in you.

What I call the "mother wound" is real. It hurts, it scars, and it can even debilitate. But Mary is real also, and she is really your mother. She can, and will, help to heal the wound, forgive your abusive or troubled mother, and find healing and peace.

Marge Steinhage Fenelon

PART ONE

LEARNING
TO FORGIVE

CHAPTER ONE

YES, YOU CAN HEAL

Now in Jerusalem by the Sheep Gate there is a pool, called in Hebrew Beth-zatha, which has five porticoes. In these lay many invalids—blind, lame, and paralyzed. One man was there who had been ill for thirty-eight years. When Jesus saw him lying there and knew that he had been there a long time, he said to him, "Do you want to be made well?" The sick man answered him, "Sir, I have no one to put me into the pool when the water is stirred up; and while I am making my way, someone else steps down ahead of me." Jesus said to him, "Stand up, take your mat and walk." At once the man was made well, and he took up his mat and began to walk.

—JOHN 5:2–9

Do you want to be made well?

That is what Jesus asked the sick man at the Sheep Gate (called Bethesda in Hebrew). The man had been ill for thirty-eight years. The blind, lame, crippled, and sick would go to the healing pool and immerse themselves—or have someone else immerse them—in the healing waters. But the sick man had no one to help him.

It is interesting that our Lord asked the man if he wanted to be well. Wouldn't it seem obvious that he wanted healing since he had been hurting for decades? Why else would he have been there?

And, since Jesus is God, he already knew whether or not the man desired a cure. He knows what is in the heart of every human being. He did not need to ask because he knew; he asked for the man's sake rather than his own. He wanted the man to examine himself and decide whether or not he wanted to be well. He wanted the sick man to participate in his own healing.

Do you want to be made well?

Believe it or not, for a very long time, my answer to that question was no. I was afraid of what it would take to be made well, so I preferred to stay just as I was, ignoring my pain and hiding my past.

I wanted to be vindicated, excused, hidden, and even at times patronized for the wounds I had suffered from my mother's mental illness. I wanted to be whole and free of the pain, and I wanted to feel normal in the way I assumed everyone else but me felt. I was sure that I was the only person in the world (aside from my siblings) with a mother like mine, or at least I was the only one of my friends and acquaintances. Admitting that I needed to be healed meant admitting that I was different, and I did not want that. I wanted other people to think that whatever went on in my house was just like whatever went on in any other house on my block, on my street, or even on the entire earth, for that matter.

No, I did not want to be well, not in the way that Jesus meant well, and not in the way I needed to be well. I certainly wanted to be relieved of those wounds, but I did not want to go through the work of affecting that relief. I just wanted to be rid of the whole mess. I did not want to let Jesus heal me because that would mean allowing myself to be vulnerable to the past. Pretending as though none of it had ever happened seemed to be the safer route.

That was easy to do since my mother was very gracious and active in our church and community. She volunteered for parish functions, corrected student assignments for the teachers of the parish school, and taught religious education. She joined a civil service group that, among other activities, assisted the city police during the horrible rioting that took place in the summer of 1967. For many years, she organized an annual Christmas party for orphans—complete with food, drinks, entertainment, gifts, and of course, a visit from Santa Claus. I remember riding along and sitting in the back seat of the car as she went from company to company to company, soliciting donations for the orphans. Although she ticked off a good number of people (usually on purpose), she had many friends and was well liked socially and at work. No one guessed what she was like at home.

From early on, I was aware that my mom was somehow broken, and I had mixed feelings about it. At times, I would become angry at her behavior because I thought she should know better. After all, she was the adult. Right? At other times, I felt sorry for her because it seemed as though she did not know better, or at least was incapable of acting better. There even were times when she seemed genuinely contrite for her actions, giving me hope that she would change her ways. Then things would turn around again, dashing my hopes. As a child, I did not understand that mental illness—and the emotional turmoil related to it—is an insidious thing that can disappear and reappear at the blink of an eye.

Even if I had tried to share my secret, I doubted that anyone would have believed me. My mother was always convinced that I was somehow up to no good and tried to convince others of the same. I think she was projecting her own sinfulness on me, and there were many times she tattled on me to the priest or my youth leader about some fictitious or imagined sin I had committed. Oddly, she bought clothes for me that were on the outer fringe of being modest and insisted I wear them. When I wouldn't, she would become furious. While she frequently accused me of being sexually illicit, she herself struggled with infidelity for most of her married life. I sometimes was required to accompany my mother and one of her boyfriends on dates—even once to a parish May Crowning! It was humiliating and confusing all at the same time.

Mom seemed unable to understand the seriousness and consequences of her actions. One can hide such a sin for only so long, and eventually my dad discovered my mom's affairs. There followed a series of counseling sessions, and things seemed to get better. I was grateful to Mom for admitting her guilt and recommitting to her marriage and wanted to tell her so. I found the Scripture passage in which Jesus forgives the adulteress and showed it to my mother, anticipating that it would offer her hope and a chance for healing. She read the passage, threw the Bible down, and berated me for having accused her of being an adulteress. This kind of scene occurred many times about many different things over the years. In her mental and emotional state, my mother never seemed to be able to acknowledge or recall any of her wrongdoings.

I came close to asking for help once. The school's annual Christmas play was drawing near, and each student in our class was asked to bring two dozen cookies for the social afterward. When I passed the request on to my mother, she scolded me for the inconvenience and refused to bake the cookies. So, the next day, as the teacher was tallying the number of cookies that would be donated, I made up an excuse about my dad not getting paid and our having no more flour in the house to bake cookies. I felt stupid because all the other moms were glad to contribute. The teacher promptly went back to my mother with this news. I can still hear them laughing and my mother saying, "I have no idea how she came up with that!"

My mother promised the cookies and delivered them herself to my teacher. That was the end of my search for help. From that moment on, I decided I would simply keep it to myself.

Unlike the man beside the pool of Bethesda, I did not want to be well. At least I did not want to be made well—there is a difference. Yet, the two of us did have something in common: we could not get to the healing waters on our own. When Jesus asked the sick man whether he wanted to be made well, he was really measuring the man's faith. It is much like asking, "Do you trust me?" He wanted the sick man to realize and truly feel his trust in him. I had faith in Jesus, but not the kind I needed to surrender my wounds to him.

So I hid them away and pretended that they were not there. At times, I even hid myself, and one of the places I went to hide was a small, white shrine dedicated to Mary. It was a Schoenstatt Marian Shrine, and it had been built on the playground of my elementary school. When I was in first grade, one of my teachers introduced me to the shrine. Despite the chaos I faced at home, I frequently got very homesick at school. One day, probably to coax me out of my tears, the gentle Sister of Mary took me out of the classroom, down the hall, out onto the playground, and into the shrine. From the moment Sister opened the door, I felt at home.

Quite literally, I was at home. A picture of Mary holding the Child Jesus in her arms was enshrined above the altar. It was the exact same picture of Mary that hung above my couch at home! At that instant, I believed that the Sisters had hung it there just for me (oh, the mind of a six-year-old!), so I would no longer get homesick. Of course, I soon learned that the picture was not a copy of mine at home but rather the opposite. Originally titled *Refuge of Sinners*, it had been renamed by the International Apostolic Movement of Schoenstatt as *Mother Thrice Admirable, Queen and Victress of Schoenstatt*. That picture and the movement's founder, Fr. Joseph Kentenich, would play a vital role in my life (as I wrote about in the Introduction).

After that day, I visited the shrine as often as I could. For the most part, I just sat there. Sometimes I would do my best to say the rosary, even though I did not fully know how. But, usually, I just sat and stared up at that picture and relished the peace and quiet of the shrine. There was a lot of conflict in my childhood home—between my parents and us siblings as well—and the shrine was void of the bickering, cursing, uneasiness, and noise at home. I felt safe there, and I was soothed by looking into the Blessed Mother's eyes. I loved examining every feature of her face, her hands, her veil. And I loved gazing at the baby Jesus nestled snugly in her arms. I felt protected and loved.

I was too young to understand Marian theology—or to even be aware that such a thing existed, for that matter—but I was not too young to sense that somehow the answer to my healing was in that shrine. More specifically, the answer to my healing was in Mary. There was no vision, no locution, no sudden revelation. Instead, it was a slow, subtle, and simple knowing that she had something I needed. And I kept wanting more and more of it. Looking back, I realize that in the Marian Shrine, I had met the person who would move me closer to the pool of Bethesda. Her name is Mary. Here is the most amazing part of my discovery. Mary moved me closer to the pool, and she is ready to move you closer, as well.

Do you want to be well? Do you really want to be well? Are you ready to go through the work of affecting that healing? I think you are; otherwise, you never would have picked up this book.

Read the Scripture passage again, this time slowly and keeping in mind what Jesus means by, "Do you want to be made well?" Put yourself in the place of the sick man. See the pool, listen to the splash of its waters, and hear the rejoicing voices of the others being cured there. Then, look into our Lord's eyes and hear him speak to you.

On most of the occasions in which Jesus healed someone, the cure was a question of faith. Jesus wanted the person to recognize his faith and trust in him. That was true of the sick man at Bethesda.

Now consider the two blind men that our Lord healed on the road near Capernaum. He had just left the home of the Jewish official, Jairus, where he had brought the official's twelve-year-old daughter back to life. Two blind men approached him along the road, begging to be healed.

"Son of David, have pity on us," they cried out to him.

Jesus responded, "Do you believe that I can do this?"

As with the man at Bethesda, Jesus wanted to measure the blind men's faith. He wanted an admission of their *trust* in him.

The men answered, "Yes, Lord."

Then Jesus touched their eyes and told them, "Let it be done for you according to your faith."

Jesus is saying the same thing to you. Let it be done according to your faith.

You will be healed if you believe that you will be healed. It takes great courage to have faith like that.

Mary had the courage, and she had that kind of faith. When the Angel Gabriel appeared to her at the Annunciation, she was afraid and confused. God wanted something of her that she considered to be beyond her capacity. He wanted her to become the Mother of his

Son. Not only was that a daunting task in and of itself, but Mary was a virgin. Motherhood, in the physical sense, was impossible. How did she respond?

> Mary said to the angel, "How can this be, since I am a virgin?" The angel said to her, "The Holy Spirit will come upon you, and the power of the Most High will overshadow you; therefore the child to be born will be holy; he will be called Son of God. And now, your relative Elizabeth in her old age has also conceived a son; and this is the sixth month for her who was said to be barren. For nothing will be impossible with God." Then Mary said, "Here am I, the servant of the Lord; let it be with me according to your word." Then the angel departed from her. (Luke 1:34–38)

Mary was not to be healed, but she was about to be changed in a drastic way. She had only one question, "How can this be?" Once Gabriel assured her that it would be done by God's power, Mary's only concern became following God's will. "Let it be with me according to your word." In courageous faith and trust, Mary allowed God to transform her.

Healing from the woundedness caused by your mother will change you in a drastic way as well. Perhaps you are afraid, as Mary was when the angel appeared to her. Certainly, there are times when you have been, and will be, confused like Mary was. But if you allow him to, our Lord will transform you, not in making you Mother of God, but in making you the whole and healed person you were meant to be.

But first, he wants you to admit that you want to be well.

CHAPTER TWO

WHY IS MARY THE ANSWER?

In dangers, in doubts, in difficulties, think of Mary, call upon Mary. Let not her name depart from your lips, never suffer it to leave your heart. And that you may obtain the assistance of her prayer, neglect not to walk in her footsteps. With her for guide, you shall never go astray; while invoking her, you shall never lose heart; so long as she is in your mind, you are safe from deception; while she holds your hand, you cannot fall; under her protection you have nothing to fear; if she walks before you, you shall not grow weary; if she shows you favor, you shall reach the goal."

—St. Bernard of Clairvaux

The above is one of my favorite quotes about the Blessed Virgin Mary. In it, St. Bernard gives such hope to anyone who calls upon her for help, assuring them that their pleas will not only be heard but answered. That can be hard to fathom if you struggle in your relationship with Mary. It can be even harder if you have no relationship with her at all.

Nearly every time I do public speaking, I am approached after my presentation by someone who confides in me that they "just don't get that Mary thing." My heart breaks for them because I want them to have the kind of relationship I have with her. There is never enough time then and there to help them, but I do my best on the spot to offer a few words of encouragement or advice. Then I hand them one of my business cards and ask them to follow up with me by email so that I can give them more support. Often, they do; sometimes they do not. Either way, I make certain to pray for them, placing them into the care of Our Lady.

Why are there so many people who "don't get that Mary thing?" Based on my own experiences and opinion, I believe it is usually one of three causes or a combination of them.

First is the tendency to have placed Mary on such a high pedestal that she becomes unreachable. Without a doubt, she deserves honor and veneration, and the Church has practiced this since the first century.[1] When the angel Gabriel appeared to her, asking that she consent to becoming the Mother of the Savior, he referred to her as the "favored one" (see Luke 1:28). That is because Mary was chosen by God himself from among all women from all eternity to conceive and bear his Son. She was born without the stain of original sin and never committed a sin. She was the first and most perfect disciple of Christ and thus is the model for all Christians. She acknowledged her place of honor when she spoke her Magnificat to her cousin Elizabeth, saying, "from now on all generations will call me blessed" (see Luke 1:48).

Yes, Mary is indeed worthy of acclaim, but, consequently, we can see her as so perfect and holy that we dare not approach her. She remains a distant, untouchable figure. We might honor her, but we cannot relate to her.

Second is the false notion that devotion to Mary gets in the way of our devotion to Christ. There are many who think that venerating and praying to our Lady somehow offends our Lord and hovers on the edge of idolatry. This could not be further from the truth. The fact is that we venerate Mary but do not worship her. Our worship is for God alone. We honor Mary because she is the Mother of God. Additionally, she is part of the communion of saints, which is the term used for the entire Church—those who are still living and those who are deceased.

> We believe in the communion of all the faithful of Christ, those who are pilgrims on earth, the dead who are attaining their purification, and the blessed in heaven, all together forming one Church; and we believe that in this communion the merciful love of God and His saints is ever listening to our prayers, as Jesus told us: Ask and you will receive.[2]

The Church also teaches that others in the communion of saints—including those who have passed away and gone to heaven—have the ability to pray to God for our intentions.

> The intercession of the saints. "Being more closely united to Christ, those who dwell in heaven fix the whole Church more firmly in holiness.... They do not cease to intercede with the Father for us, as they proffer the merits which they acquired on earth through the one mediator between God and men, Christ Jesus.... So by their fraternal concern is our weakness greatly helped." (*CCC*, 956)

When we pray to Mary, we're asking her to intercede for us to her Son, and it's with the understanding that she will not and cannot usurp God's will. She does not grant things directly or make things happen of her own accord. It is not unlike asking a friend to pray for a special intention of ours. They pray on our behalf as Jesus directed during his ministry on earth. He told us, "Ask and it will be given to you; seek and you will find; knock and the door will be opened to you. For everyone who asks, receives; and the one who seeks, finds; and to the one who knocks, the door will be opened" (Matthew 7:7–8, NABRE).

In Mary's case, her intercessory power is far stronger because she is Jesus's mother. This was explained in a very beautiful way in the Vatican Council II document, *Lumen Gentium*.

> After this manner the Blessed Virgin advanced in her pilgrimage of faith, and faithfully persevered in her union with her Son unto the cross, where she stood, in keeping with the divine plan, grieving exceedingly with her only begotten Son, uniting herself with a maternal heart with His sacrifice, and lovingly consenting to the immolation of this Victim which she herself had brought forth. Finally, she was given by the same Christ Jesus dying on the cross as a mother to His disciple with these words: "Woman, behold thy son."[3]

As Catholics, we believe that when Jesus gave his mother and the apostle John to each other, he saw John as representative of all humankind. Therefore, he placed not only the apostle himself into Mary's care, but all of us along with him. That is also true in reverse. When Jesus asked John to care for his mother, he was asking us to care for her as well. And so it is completely right that we should seek her help in times of need. From the cross, Jesus gave his mother to us as intercessor.

There is more. Our Lord's action at his death has even deeper meaning for us. The Catholic Church teaches that Mary is the mother of all human beings "in the order of grace." That term may sound strange at first, but once we take it apart and examine it, you will see how truly wonderful it is. There are three paragraphs in the *Catechism of the Catholic Church* that will help.

The first refers to Mary as the Church's model of faith and charity:

> By her complete adherence to the Father's will, to his Son's redemptive work, and to every prompting of the Holy Spirit, the Virgin Mary is the Church's model of faith and charity. Thus she is a "preeminent and…wholly unique member of the Church"; indeed, she is the "exemplary realization" (*typus*) of the Church. (*CCC*, 967)

Mary is what the Church should be—completely faithful to God and dedicated to the salvation of all mankind.

But that's not all.

> Her role in relation to the Church and to all humanity goes still further. "In a wholly singular way she cooperated by her obedience, faith, hope, and burning charity in the Savior's work of restoring supernatural life to souls. For this reason she is a mother to us in the order of grace." (*CCC*, 968)

Mary cares for our souls in a way that no human mother ever could—even the most wonderful, loving one! It is that burning charity that motivates her to work tirelessly for our salvation. She wants our salvation so desperately that she appeared many times over the centuries, sharing messages of hope and calling for prayer and conversion. When she appeared to two children on September 19, 1846, in La Salette, France, our Lady told them, "I want that everybody be saved, the good as well as the bad. I am the Mother of Love, the Mother of all; you are all my children. Therefore, I wish you all to be saved. This is the reason I am inviting the entire world to prayer."[4] Her desire that all should be saved is born of a mother's deep and lasting love for her children.

The *Catechism* puts it this way:

> This motherhood of Mary in the order of grace continues uninterruptedly from the consent which she loyally gave at the Annunciation and which she sustained without wavering beneath the cross, until the eternal fulfillment of all the elect. Taken up to heaven she did not lay aside this saving office but by her manifold intercession continues to bring us the gifts of eternal salvation.… Therefore the Blessed Virgin is invoked in the Church under the titles of Advocate, Helper, Benefactress, and Mediatrix. (*CCC*, 969)

Fr. Joseph Kentenich said that when Mary gave her yes to being Jesus's mother at the Annunciation, she gave her yes to being our mother as well. In a series of Lenten homilies that Fr. Kentenich prepared for a Milwaukee parish in 1954, he wrote:

> This mother heart began to beat for us maternally at the moment she pronounced her fiat, at the moment it began to beat for our Lord. The instant she became the physical Mother of the Head of the Mystical Body she also became the spiritual Mother of the members of Christ and became my Mother, too. Her heart bled spiritually for me at the foot of the Cross.[5]

You might say that she spiritually conceived us in her womb at that moment. What an incredible act of love! Mary was our mother before we even existed. Her yes to motherhood was not just for our Lord, not just for the people who lived at that time, but for the people who have, do, and will live for all time. Her love for God extended to all of his children and is so tremendous that it is limitless.

As our mother, she cares about every aspect of our lives, past, present, and future. She cares about our joys and sorrows, successes and failures, dreams and desires. She cares about where we have been and where we are going. She cares about who we are and who we would like to become. She cares about the seemingly insignificant details of our daily routines and the huge life events. She cares about all that is important to us and even about what is not so important. She cares about everything.

Everything includes our pain. Good mothers want nothing more than to ease the pain of their children. In fact, they would rather endure the pain themselves than see their children suffer with it. That is exactly the kind of good mother Mary is—she would rather endure the pain herself than to see us suffer. And so she cares about the pain we bear because of the way we have been treated and hurt by our mothers. She cares not only about the fact that the pain is there, but also about how to help us heal from it. She loves us and wants to become the instrument of our healing. And she will, if we allow her. She can, and will, intercede for us to her Son, the ultimate healer. Mary is our mother in a very real way, and because of that, she loves us in a very real and sustaining way.

Mary is the answer to our need for healing. But our relationship with our natural mothers can get in the way. I learned this from Fr. Kentenich, and it has proven true in my own life and in the lives of other people I know as well. "A religious experience involving the [heavenly] Father presupposes positive experiences with a father in the natural order. A religious experience involving the Mother [Mary] normally presupposes a corresponding experience in the natural order," Fr. Kentenich said.[6] In other words, the way in which we relate to God the Father and Blessed Mother Mary is heavily dependent on the way we relate to our earthly father and mother.

If we have had a negative mothering experience on the human level, it is tough to open our hearts to a positive mothering experience from Mary. If we have not been close to our physical mothers, it is more challenging to become close to our spiritual mother. If we have been abused or neglected, we may even be afraid to draw close to Mary. You could say that the way we feel about our physical mothers conditions us to feel the same way about Mary. Additionally, Fr. Kentenich taught that, in order to fully heal our mother wounds, we can—and must—make up for what we lacked growing up.[7] We must replace the negative mothering experiences with good ones in one or both of these ways: Attach ourselves to a positive mother figure or become the mother we wish we had had. Mary is the answer for fulfilling both of those conditions.

Mary can help you to find and attach to a solid, loving mother figure on the natural level. If you ask her, she will guide you to them. Perhaps she is a mentor, older friend, or consecrated religious. I was fortunate to have many positive mother figures over the years—a friend's mom, a youth leader, a Schoenstatt Sister of Mary, and a couple of close friends who are older than me. You can bet I've not been the perfect mother myself, but I've had all these examples—positive *and* negative (my mother)—to help me be a mother to my own children in the way I'd wished my mother had been to me. Finally, because of Fr. Kentenich's keenness in consecrating me to the Blessed Virgin, I have been in Mary's motherly care since I was a baby.

No matter what you lack from your childhood, it can be recovered with the Blessed Virgin's help. Mary is the answer.

CHAPTER THREE

IT'S OKAY TO LOOK BACK

If an ear is to grow or a flower blossom, there are times which cannot be forced; for the birth of a human being, nine months are required; to write a book or a worthy piece of music, years must often be spent in patient searching. This is also the law of the spirit.... To encounter the mystery takes patience, inner purification, silence and waiting.[8]

—POPE ST. JOHN PAUL II; GENERAL AUDIENCE,

JULY 26, 2000

Like the development of a human being, healing is a process that cannot be forced. It is very much like composing a musical score, crafting an artwork, or writing a book. It requires patient searching, inner purification, silence, and waiting.

For many, many years after I moved out of my mother's house, I had nightmares. I would wake up in the middle of the night, terrified, in a cold sweat, and unsure of where I was at first. I would be positive that she had somehow crept into my bedroom and was about to do me harm. In my sleep, I would relive my experiences with my mother and would often dream that my father had been buried alive—probably because I so desperately longed to have him back. It would take a while for me to settle down and realize that I was indeed safe and that Dad had undergone a proper burial and was resting at peace in God's hands. This continued well into the first decade of my marriage. I also would jump and scream bloody murder if anyone entered the room or approached me unexpectedly. Although I am better than I was, I still have a slight tendency to do that. Thanks be to God I have a husband who has been patient, caring, and willing to put up with my odd reactions. My kids have accepted it as well, even though they were not aware of the cause of my quirks until they reached adulthood.

Part of the reason for this, I think, is that it is just my nature to be easily startled. The other part of the reason is growing up with fear over what would come next from my mother or when the next argument would erupt between my mother and father. My mother's verbal attacks were unprovoked and came out of nowhere. She could switch instantaneously from being kind and loving to threatening and screaming obscenities at me. I never learned what set her off or how to avoid her rages and insults. She also had a peculiar way of showing up suddenly; everything she did was for attention and shock value. After my father died, my mother brought her boyfriend to live with us. He was an unusual character and had a knack for appearing at my bedroom door out of the blue. Although he never harmed me, he made me uneasy. And so I was constantly on guard.

My remedy for this was to pray. I prayed that the memories would just go away and never come back. I figured that, if I gave it all to God and then ignored the past, it would all go away. Then, I would quash the memories and get busy with something—anything—that would occupy my mind elsewhere. Well, it was right of me to pray—none of us can do a thing without God's grace—but I learned that the past will not go away by ignoring it. Eventually, it has to come out and be dealt with.

I did manage to repress my memories for a good long time. I thought I was doing pretty well until one day when my children were very small. It was one of those days when everything and nothing was going wrong all at the same time. When you have kids, you have chaos, and that is to be expected. I no longer recall specifically what set me off, but I found myself in inconsolable tears. I felt as though my whole world was falling apart, and yet nothing especially serious or sad had happened. Then I realized that what was really bothering me was not my children, but rather my own childhood memories and emotions dredged up by my kids simply being kids.

Something a wise priest had told me years before came to my mind. I loved this Schoenstatt father for his kind manner and sought his counsel on many matters, including my secrets involving my mother. Father had cautioned me that having children of my own likely would bring back the painful and scary memories of my childhood. "It could be that you relive those times after your own children are born. Seeing them will remind you of yourself as a child, and it could become very difficult. Do not be afraid of that. Accept it and work with it," he said.

He knew what he was talking about, because that is exactly what ended up happening. I knew then that I would have to face my past head-on. If I did not turn around and take a long, hard look at the past, it would continue to creep up on me and disturb my peace of mind. If I were going to move forward, I would have to compel myself to look backward. I also knew that I would have to do it purposefully and under guidance. That's not all. I would need much prayer, frequent reception of the sacraments, God's grace, and the protection and nurturing of the Blessed Virgin Mary. I could not possibly do it alone.

I continued intense spiritual direction. I also went to a professional counselor, someone who had the specialized training to show me how to handle the effects of my mother's abusiveness and cope with the bad memories. At the time, I did not have a ton of choices because our health insurance limited my options. But I did manage to find a decent Christian counselor who taught me one of the most important lessons of my life:

The past can only hurt you if you let it.

Sounds simple in principle, but it is complicated to apply. The counselor taught me something he called "mindfulness."[9] In a nutshell, it is a method of focusing on the here and now and separating the past from the present and the other from the self. Here is what it looks like in action. When a bad memory surfaced and my emotions began to get out of control, I was to stop, call upon God's grace, and focus on something in my immediate environment, preferably something pleasant. If I was outdoors, it might be the leaves on a tree rustling in the wind. If indoors, it might be a flowering plant or picture of a religious figure. The idea was to pause and separate what was then from what is now. In doing this, I would bring myself to realize that I was not trapped in my childhood. Rather, I was a grown adult with my own life and access to God's grace and Mary's protection. My mother was no longer standing next to me, swearing and calling me names. She could not harm me; she was only a memory.

It was not easy, but I finally mastered it. I got to the point of being able to look back and say, "Ugh. That was terrible, but I am safe now. She can only hurt me if I let her, and I won't let her." The best part is that the more often I practiced the mindfulness technique, the greater my awareness of Mary as my true, loving mother became, and the deeper my love for her grew.

In my thinking, this is akin to what St. John of the Cross wrote about in *Ascent of Mount Carmel*. The book is about spiritual aestheticism and growing to such a level of spiritual perfection that one becomes completely united with God. One of the ways to do that is to put the memory aside and focus totally on God to the point that it seems as if nothing else existed—not even oneself! This is often referred to as purification of the memory. While striving for this perfection, your memory is purged of all worldly things, all worries, temptations, needs, people, tasks, distractions, fears, desires, ambitions, and so on. There is only…God.

> This is our task now with the memory. We must draw it away
> from its natural props and capacities and raise it above itself
> (above all distinct knowledge and apprehensible possession)
> to supreme hope in the incomprehensible God.[10]

It is inevitable that memories of the past will arise; it is how we deal with them that makes the difference. St. John of the Cross stated that "God does not destroy, but perfects nature."[11] If we turn our looking back over to God, he will see to it that we are given the grace to handle it. Without grace, my memories would have led me to an ugly place and left me there.

St. John cautioned that the devil can use our memories to gain influence over our souls. "For he can add to its knowledge other forms, ideas, and reasonings, and by means of them move it to pride, avarice, anger, envy, etc., and insert unjust hatred, vain love, and many kinds of delusions."[12]

Not only can the demons mess with our minds, but we can mess with our own minds as well. Dr. Susan Muto, Dean of the Epiphany Academy of Formative Spirituality, addressed this in her book *John of the Cross for Today: The Ascent*. Dr. Muto has studied the writings of St. John of the Cross and applied them to modern, everyday life.

She writes, "The memory can play tricks on us. What is false seems true after enough rationalization, what is doubtful, certain. Emotions are stirred up as we return in memory to the sensate objects and stimulating events. Suddenly, we feel sorrowful, fearful, hateful, vain."[13]

Yes, we need to face our memories, but if we obsess over them, continuously replay them, or fear them, we can end up making things seem worse than they actually were.

To prevent tampering with our memories—either by demonic influence or our own humanness—we need to turn them over to God and invoke the Holy Spirit to guide us. That will help to safeguard both our memories and our souls.

"For God's Spirit makes them know what must be known and ignore what must be ignored, remember what ought to be remembered—with or without form—and forget what ought to be forgotten, and makes them love what they ought to love, and keeps them from loving what is not in God," St. John of the Cross writes.[14]

It seems to me that St. John's modus of purification of the memory takes my former counselor's method of mindfulness to a higher, more spiritual level. Mindfulness stops the process of being pulled back in time while purification elevates the memories and draws one closer to God. Through the working of the Holy Spirit, we are lifted out of the abyss and into the present moment and filled with God's love and grace. St. Paul said it so well in his letter to the Corinthians, "But whoever is joined to the Lord becomes one spirit with him" (1 Corinthians 6:17, NABRE)

For me, an essential component to purifying my memory rested in my relationship with Mary. She had always been there for me, and I had always felt safe in her presence when I prayed or visited her shrine. I desperately needed a mother, and I thank God for giving me the grace to open my heart to her. I also thank her for opening her heart to me. She somehow made me aware of her nearness, and I know that she protected me from many dangerous situations, both spiritually and physically. When I held on to her hand, figuratively speaking, the memories were not so scary. Often, I would just look at her picture, having no words to say, and not really understanding what I was feeling, but it did not matter. Merely spending time with her was soothing.

There is a prayer I learned as a young child that has been a great help to me. It is a prayer of consecration, or surrender of oneself, to the Blessed Virgin Mary. It was composed by the Jesuit Nicolaus Zucchi in the seventeenth century and has become a customary prayer of the Schoenstatt Movement that they refer to as "The Little Consecration." Whenever I said that prayer, I felt as though Mary was surrounding me with an impenetrable shield. I felt secure and loved. I still do, and I say it often. I would like to pass it on to you in hope that, as your relationship with her grows, you will find solace and strength in this prayer also.

> THE LITTLE CONSECRATION
> My Queen, My Mother,
> I give myself entirely to you.
> And to show my devotion to you,
> I consecrate to you this day,
> My eyes, my ears, my mouth, my heart,
> My entire self without reserve.
> As I am your own, my good Mother,
> Guard me and defend me
> As your property and possession. Amen.

Fr. Kentenich spoke of the Marian consecration in terms of an exchange of hearts with Mary. Once we give our hearts to her, she assists in helping us to let go of all the bad memories and their ensuing fears—compulsions, as he calls them—so that we may grow in our love for God. In a series of Lenten homilies given in Milwaukee, Wisconsin, in 1954, he said, "A heart is generous and free when its love for Mary and God is free from internal and external compulsion, free from any kind of human fear, and when it gives itself only and always to dependence on the partner in love."[15] That is exactly what we want: hearts that are generous and free, untethered from the pain and agony of the past. The only way to untether them is to look back at them, acknowledge them, accept them, digest them, and let go of them in complete surrender to God. Once we do that, we can look to the future with hope.

Let me end this chapter with a quote that truly inspires me, and I think it will inspire you also. It is taken from the International Theological Commission's document *Memory and Reconciliation: The Church and the Faults of the Past.*

"The past is grasped in the potentialities which it discloses, in the stimulus it offers to modify the present. Memory becomes capable of giving rise to a new future."[16]

CHAPTER FOUR

YOU ARE A CHILD OF GOD

It is better to be the child of God than king of the whole world.[17]

—ST. ALOYSIUS GONZAGA

When I was in second grade, we had three reading groups, and students were assigned to a group depending on their reading skills. The advanced readers belonged to Group 1, average readers to Group 2, and kids who were slower readers to Group 3. I was assigned to Group 2. I was okay with that. In fact, I never thought I had much skill in general.

One day, my teacher took me aside during reading class.

"Margaret, I'm moving you to Group 1 because I think you can read a whole lot better than you think you can," she said.

I was immediately placed in Group 1, and my reading level—as well as my love for reading—took off like a rocket. That is because my teacher believed in me even when I did not believe in myself.

The same kind of thing happened when I was in fifth grade. Our school held a writing contest, and I wanted to enter. I did not really believe I could win, but I wrote a story anyway. I liked to write and figured this was as good a reason as any to put my pen to paper. I still remember the basics of the story. It was about a girl who had fallen into a well and ended up in leg braces because she had injured her legs to the point that they were no longer useful. I remember that I got the idea for the story from a painting of a Victorian-era girl in leg braces, but I do not clearly remember who had given it to me. Perhaps the contest committee had handed out pictures as story starters for the contestants. I had asked my dad to help me work out the logistics of the accident so that my story would be plausible. He gladly agreed, even drawing sketches so that I could envision for myself how the girl had been injured. I worked hard and wrote what I thought was a decent story.

I turned it in, convinced that I hadn't a chance in the world of winning the contest. I was so sure I'd lose that I never told my mother and father that the winners would be announced at the next Home and School Association meeting and that all contestants and their parents were encouraged to attend. Besides, I knew my mom would get upset with me for asking her to go, and my dad worked second shift at the time. The next day, the school principal stopped me on my way into the building. She wanted to congratulate me and give me my prize. I had won first place! Again, it was a case of others seeing in me what I did not—could not—see myself.

Why couldn't I see my own value? I think it is because I was afraid to see it. I was afraid to succeed or be honored for anything. Any success, achievement, or milestone I experienced set my mother off. It struck a vicious aggression in her that came out in verbal attacks and intentional embarrassment. Sometimes, it would come in a brief outburst. Other times, it would go on for hours, even over the course of days. After my high school graduation ceremony, the graduates lined up in the hallway so that attendees could pass by and offer their congratulations. It was an extremely emotional event for me, made extra difficult by my father's recent death. He had died when I was a sophomore, leaving me all alone with my mother. My heart ached at the thought of Dad's absence from my high school graduation. In the midst of it all, my mother stormed up to me. As soon as I saw her approaching, I knew it was going to be bad. Sure enough, she laid into me, cursing me out and mimicking my crying. For me, it was quite a usual thing to expect from my mother. My fellow graduates and bystanders, however, were shocked. I was so embarrassed that I wanted to just disappear.

Ironically, my mother loved to show me off to her friends and coworkers. She would take me to her workplace or introduce me at an event, glowing over me and telling people, "That's my baby!" I remained silent and smiled like a good little girl. In my grade school, we had the tradition of having a May Queen and May King for the annual parish festival. They were chosen by how many raffle tickets they had sold, and by golly, Mom made sure I was the winner. All was well until we got home after the festival. Then the snide remarks and hateful glares broke loose. She encouraged me to join clubs, become involved in projects, or try out for the plays at my high school. But afterwards? Bang! She would criticize, insult, and curse me. As a child and teen, I could never figure out why she behaved that way. As an adult looking back, I can only guess that she was in an ongoing state of emotional turmoil, with misguided mothering instincts at odds with the immature and abused child within her.

Because of my mother's resentment of me, I developed a fear of success that I carried into adulthood. I worked at diminishing it, but it always was an uphill battle. Granted, I also had apprehensions about failing—most people do—but I was far more afraid of succeeding. Despite that, I managed to do well in college. I was fortunate enough to have had professors who thought highly of me and were exceptionally encouraging. Plus, I had moved away from my mother to another city. She persisted in trying to torment me with harassing phone calls and taunting when I would go home to visit, but once the phone was hung up or the visit ended, I could turn my attention to earning my degree. Still, it took me a few years after college to gather the courage to practice my profession (journalism) and more than a decade after that to write my first book.

That itself is a funny story. I had been writing short essays for the Schoenstatt Movement's internal monthly magazine and, over time, accumulated a couple hundred of them. I received frequent positive response from people who read my essays, and the editor was very happy with my work. At one of the movement's events, she took me aside and told me that I should make a book out of my essays. I laughed at her.

"Sister," I said, "who in the world would be interested in that?"

"You'd be surprised," she replied. "Lots of people would. You really should do a book with your articles."

Graciously, the editor persisted. Finally, I decided that I would pursue the idea just to prove to her that she was dead wrong. My spiritual director chimed in with his support. An author himself, he even volunteered to help me self-publish the book. His only condition was that I first try to sell the manuscript to a major publishing house. I agreed, and after a number of rejections that nearly made me give up, it sold. My first book, *When's God Gonna Show Up? Daily Discoveries of the Divine* was released in 2009. The rest, as they say, is history.

Mistreatment by anyone, and especially by a parent, can leave us feeling worthless and unloved. When we feel unloved by human beings close to us, it can be difficult to feel loved by God. As you saw in my example, it can get to the point that it affects our life decisions and responses to the world around us. Rejection from others can cause us to reject ourselves. That is a natural reaction, but it is contrary to what our Lord has taught us. Even when we question ourselves, God does not question us. What I mean is this. God knows us. He knows he has given us each numerous gifts and that we are able, with his grace, to use those gifts to their full potential. I promise you that, no matter how badly you feel unsure, unloved, and unworthy, God loves you, and no one or nothing can separate you from his love.

St. Paul assures us of that in his Letter to the Romans.

> What will separate us from the love of Christ? Will anguish, or distress, or persecution, or famine, or nakedness, or peril, or the sword? As it is written: "For your sake we are being slain all the day; we are looked upon as sheep to be slaughtered." No, in all these things we conquer overwhelmingly through him who loved us. For I am convinced that neither death, nor life, nor angels, nor principalities, nor present things, nor future things, nor powers, nor height, nor depth, nor any other creature will be able to separate us from the love of God in Christ Jesus our Lord. (Romans 8:35–39, NABRE)

However, to know in our heads that God loves us and to feel it in our hearts can be two very different things. It requires the attribute of childlikeness. That is not the same as childishness. Childishness is a result of immaturity, whether it is temporary or long-term. Childish people do not have full control over their actions and emotions. They lack poise and at times, even purpose. Childlike people do have poise, purpose, and control—for the most part—over their actions and emotions. Let's face it. Everyone loses it once in a while! That is a result of the effects of original sin.

A childlike person has a heart that is both uncomplicated and wise, loving, and trusting in God as Father. A childlike person feels sheltered and safe in God's love, with a sound faith and confidence in both God and in his own strength (which has been given to him by God). He lives his life peacefully and without worry about the past or future. A truly childlike person can cope with, and even overcome, anxiety. A child knows that whatever happens to him at every moment was foreseen for him by the Father and will contribute to his formation. The childlike person's only concern is to discover what God wants from him right now.

Fr. Kentenich wrote and spoke much about childlikeness and God's love for us. He was convinced that childlikeness was the key to holy, emotionally stable life even during turbulent times. He once said, "No one loves us more tenderly and deeply than the Father. This is also and particularly true when we cannot understand his love. Can the Father show greater love than when he helps his children to become like his only-begotten Son, who hangs on the cross? He only does this to his favorite children."[18]

The most perfect example of childlikeness is the Blessed Virgin Mary. Catholic dogma of the Immaculate Conception tells us that she was born without the effects of original sin and thus was filled with grace in an unparalleled way. With the exception of Jesus himself, no soul was ever as filled with grace as Mary's was. Because of this, the early Church Fathers called her "daughter of the Father."[19] In every way, Mary had the attitude of a child, exemplifying humility, confidence, and complete surrender to the will of the Father. She learned her childlikeness from her own son. Like

Jesus, she made God's desires her own. "The entire life of Our Lady is an actualization of God's will, a constant and absolute surrender to the wish and will of the Father," Fr. Kentenich writes.[20]

In her childlikeness, Mary was so secure in God's love that, no matter what, she could and did repeat her fiat, or unconditional yes to all that God asked of her. Her complete childlikeness was a gift of the Holy Spirit, who overshadowed her at the Annunciation and again at Pentecost. The Holy Spirit is the spirit of childlikeness. Mary is the vessel of the Holy Spirit, and as such, she is the embodiment of perfect childlikeness. As I wrote about in chapter two, Mary is our Mother, and she loves us deeply. Because she is a child of God herself and loves us so very much, she wants us to experience that same joy of being a child of God. She understands how important and powerful his love is, and she knows how profoundly God loves each of us individually and uniquely. She can and will intercede for us, invoking the Holy Spirit to lead us toward sincere childlikeness.

I have often been asked how I managed to endure what I did without having become bitter or warped. My answer always is the same: Mary. I could never have survived without her. My attachment to her—or more precisely, her attachment to me—kept me going. In her tender, motherly love, she saw to it that I was made aware that I was indeed a child of God. She helped me to believe that there was meaning and purpose for everything, even though I did not know what it was at the time. When my world really started to rock, I held fast to her to steady it. I can't count the number of times things would get so bad that I'd hide in my bedroom or head outdoors to escape my mother. I would repeat the Little Consecration prayer or sing Marian songs over and over and over just to drown out mom's snarls and vulgar language. It seems that with each panicked beat my heart drew closer to Mary and, through her, to God. I am definitely not perfect. I do have some emotional scars and plenty of faults to work on. But I am working on it, and that is what counts.

That is what counts for you, too. It counts that you are working on yourself. I know that because you are reading this book right now. The next step is to pray for the desire to become childlike. If you have had a traumatic childhood, that may be the last thing you think you want. Remember, childishness is not the same as childlikeness. Childishness will lead you away from healing; childlikeness will lead you toward it.

Then, ask Mary to guide you. She will not force her way into your life; she will wait to be invited. You must open your heart and invite her. Once invited, she will never, ever give up on you. Realize, however, that even with Mary's help, nobody reaches childlikeness overnight and perhaps not even over a year or a decade. It will be a slow process because woundedness takes time to heal. Add to that the fact that we are prone to succumb to the effects of original sin, and you have got yourself an obstacle course to navigate.

You will proceed in steps going both forward and backward and at times it may seem as though you are only going backward without ever going forward. The upside is that, although it may be tough, it is not impossible. It will take prayer and persistence, but you can do it.

CHAPTER FIVE

She Is a Child of God

Indeed it is written: Everyone who sins is a slave of sin; but the slave does not abide in the house for ever. The son abides for ever. Since then we too have been granted to have been called sons according to grace, we remain in the house for ever, if we hold firm the beginning of our undertaking to the end.[21]

—St. Theodore the Studite

You might not want to hear what I am about to tell you. In fact, I think you might have a hard time believing it and might even want to close this book and never pick it up again. Please don't! Please don't because what I am about to say is the absolute truth and is essential to your healing.

Your mother is a child of God.

Do not close the book. Take a deep breath and hear me out. I know that the mere thought of your mother as a child of God can put you in turmoil, or at least aggravate you. Still, it is the truth. You might not be able to accept it right now, but you will in time. Here's the thing: God created all human beings. He is Father of all, and he loves each one unconditionally. If God is Father of all, that means that all are his children, from the most cherished saint to the most hardened sinner, and from the most ardent believer to the professed atheist. Even if at times she did not act like it, your

35

mother is a human being. She was created by God, she is loved by God, and she is a child of God.

If I could accurately guess, I would say that right now you are thinking, "Well, that's fine for *you* to say, but you didn't have *my* mother!" No, I did not have your mother. But I did have my mother, so I understand what a strange thought this might seem to be at first. Regardless of what our mothers have done (or not done), how they have behaved, or how we feel about them, they are all children of God.

Think about St. Paul. According to his own words, he was the worst sinner of them all. "This saying is trustworthy and deserves full acceptance: Christ Jesus came into the world to save sinners. Of these I am the foremost" (1 Timothy 1:15, NABRE).

Before his conversion, Paul was called Saul. Saul was a terrible sinner, persecuting and killing Christians. And yet, God sent his only begotten Son to save him by dying an excruciating death on the cross. God loved Saul even while he was slicing the throats of his other children!

Paul went on to say, "But for that reason I was mercifully treated, so that in me, as the foremost, Christ Jesus might display all his patience as an example for those who would come to believe in him for everlasting life" (1 Timothy 1:16, NABRE).

I have no doubt that Paul required a great deal of God's patience, acting as he did. Yet God showed him that patience because he had a purpose for Paul, just as he has a purpose for you as his child. And he has a purpose for your mother as his child. You may not know that purpose now, and you might never know it. But it exists. God does not create human beings randomly.

Crazy as it might sound, God not only creates human beings with a purpose, but he also creates them in his image. All of them.

Because God creates through wisdom, his creation is ordered: "You have arranged all things by measure and number and weight." The universe, created in and by the eternal Word, the "image of the invisible God," is destined for and addressed to man, himself created in the "image of God" and called to a personal relationship with God. (*CCC*, 299)

There were times when my mother's behavior became so outrageous that I actually wondered if she'd been possessed by demons. In particular, there was one night soon after my dad's funeral that I lay in bed crying because I missed him so much and felt so lost without him. With my three older siblings having moved out of the house years before, I was all alone with Mom, which did not help the situation. Suddenly, from the other side of my bedroom door came a voice that I barely recognized as my mother's. It was growly, eerie, and scared the daylights out of me. She taunted me for crying and mimicked my sobs. Then in a most terrible tone, she told me that she was glad my father was dead and that she hoped he was rotting in hell. Then she proceeded to describe to me, in gruesome detail, exactly how Dad's body would burn. This did not seem like the behavior of a human being to me.

Did she really mean what she had said? Was she acting out in her own grief and agony? I didn't know, but I seriously wondered if she had been possessed by demons and took my concerns to my spiritual director. To ease my fears, he agreed to visit Mom, and she agreed to the visit as well. That did not surprise me since she often tried to convince the priests and religious sisters in my life what a horrible sinner I was. I figured she would try to do the same with my spiritual director. However, he knew better. I do not know much about their time together, but afterward, Father told me that he'd concluded that my mother was not truly possessed, and I trusted his judgment. That calmed my fear, but I still did not feel safe with her.

Not long after that, Mom sold our house, and we moved into a duplex in a neighboring city. My bedroom in this place had no door, but rather a curtain I had put up myself. One night, I was fast asleep when I sensed a presence in the room. I held perfectly still but opened my eyes enough to check things out. In the moonlight that came through the window, I saw that it was my mother. She was standing over my bed with a butcher knife in her hand. I was afraid of what would happen if I stirred, so I tried to play it cool.

"What are you doing?' I asked her.

"Nothing," she said. She turned, left my room, put the knife back in the drawer, and went back to her own bed.

The next morning, I called my spiritual director and told him what had happened. He was adamant—I needed to move out of there immediately. If I did not have a place to go, he would find me one. He felt it was no longer safe for me to live with my mother. I made arrangements to move in with my sister and her roommates in another city almost sixty miles away. Mom was not happy about it, but I was not going to let her stop me. I would soon turn eighteen anyway, and by then there would be nothing she could do legally.

I have prayed long and hard about sharing that story in this book. It is risky for me. But it is a risk I am willing to take if it will do some good. I am hoping it will help you to see your own mother as a child of God. You see, incidents like that made it incredibly difficult for me to see my mother as a child of God. Yet she was. Head to toe, good days and bad days, Mom was—and still is—a child of God. It was her own woundedness that caused her to act that way.

Back when I was about twelve years old, I had become really angry at my mother for something she had done. I no longer remember what it was, but I do remember venting to my father. He couldn't do anything to change my mother, but he did something that changed *me*. He told me that Mom had been raised by an alcoholic father and a gambling-addicted mother. Her father, in drunken fits of rage, would beat her. Her mother would sell her belongings for gambling money, including a fancy baby doll she had received as a precious Christmas gift. Mom never got over the loss of that doll, and she carried all the horrors of her childhood with her through life. I was still afraid, and I would still get really angry at my mother for things she did. But knowing her background moved me to look at her in another way and helped me struggle for perspective and strive toward compassion for her. She was a product of her past, and she would not be able to give me what she had not received from her mother.

You, too, need to struggle for perspective and strive toward compassion with your own mother. I will bet that knowing more about her background will help you. If you cannot speak with her directly, then maybe you can talk to people who had known her as a child, or at least for the long-term. There are all kinds of ways online to trace a person's life history, and I wonder if that might assist you. If you can't discover her background, then you can't. It could be that you can't find anyone who knew your mother that well or that you can't bring yourself to look into her background because it's too painful. Even so, you owe her the benefit of the doubt that there is something in her background that has caused her to be the way she is. A person cannot give what they have not received, and I have told my own children this many times. If our upbringing has been devoid of real love, support, and nurturing, we will not be able to give it to others. At least not of our own volition. That is true for your mom, too.

Whether or not you understand your mother, please do surrender her and all her thoughts, words, and actions to God—even the ones that cut right through you and leave you writhing in pain. It will help you in two ways: First, it will help you to let go of your anger and to think more clearly before reacting or responding. Second, it will solicit God's grace for you, but also for your mom. I will say it again: Your mother is a child of God. Because of that, he takes great interest in everything she does. He also takes great interest in everything that you do or that is done to you. He loves you both deeply.

> With creation, God does not abandon his creatures to themselves. He not only gives them being and existence, but also, and at every moment, upholds and sustains them in being, enables them to act and brings them to their final end. Recognizing this utter dependence with respect to the Creator is a source of wisdom and freedom, of joy and confidence." (*CCC*, 301)

God has given each of us the gift of free will, and he allows us to use it in any way we want. But great gifts also come with great responsibility. With free will, we have the right to choose between godly and ungodly ways. On the flip side, we have the responsibility to choose good over evil. If we do not, we must accept the consequences. Therefore, your mom can make her choices about how she treats you. By the same token, you can make your choices about how you respond to her. God allows this in his infinite wisdom, love, and mercy. But God does not just dole out free will and then turn his back on his children. He continues to love, uphold, and sustain them. God will uphold and sustain you in your trials. If you surrender your mom to God as his child, he will sustain and uphold her as well.

I love this passage from the book of Wisdom, and I think it is fitting to quote it here.

> For you love all things that exist, and detest none of the things that you have made; for you would not have made anything if you had hated it. How would anything have endured, if you had not willed it? Or how would anything not called forth by you have been preserved? You spare all things, for they are yours, O Lord, you who love the living. (Wisdom 11:24–26, NABRE)

There is another aspect to all this. For as much as God is a loving and merciful God, he is also a just God. Sure, we have free will, but we also must answer for how we choose to use it. In his Letter to the Colossians, St. Paul promised, "For the wrongdoer will receive recompense for the wrong he committed, and there is no partiality" (Colossians 3:25, NABRE). I knew that my mom would someday have to answer for her behavior and that it was not for me to judge how or when that would take place.

A story my dad told me when I was young helped me to see that we must not judge others nor wish to have revenge for injustice against us. We never know their circumstances, the suffering they bear inside, or God's plan for them.

Dad was a foreman at a steel factory. There was a fellow employee, he told me, that wronged him in a big way. Dad never said how he had been wronged by this fellow, only that it was serious and made him angry. He was so angry that he wished there was a way to get the guy back. One day on the job, Dad was summoned for an emergency. A four-ton steel coil had fallen from the crane and landed on one of the men. As foreman, it was my father's responsibility to handle the situation and accompany the injured person to the hospital. When Dad arrived at the scene, he was told that the coil had crushed and severed the man's arm at the elbow. The man who had been hurt was the same man that had wronged my father. Dad had to retrieve the arm, wrap it in newspaper, and ride in the ambulance along with the man.

"No matter how badly someone had wronged you," Dad told me, "never seek revenge. You never know what God has planned for that person."

Of course, the man did not lose his arm because he'd done wrong to my Dad—God doesn't work that way—but the man's accident was a stark reminder to my father that we must be charitable toward everyone, even our enemies. This is the caution that St. Paul gave to the Romans: "Never take your own revenge, beloved, but leave room for the wrath of God, for it is written, 'Vengeance is mine, I will repay,' says the Lord" (Romans 12:19, NABRE). Dad's example struck home with me, and I have always done my best to stick to it.

Many years ago, I came across a psalm that has been a huge help to me in this regard. I was grieved and upset over something someone had done to me. I needed answers about how to move forward, so I took out my Bible. I prayed, asking God to show me the answer when I opened the book. I closed my eyes, set the Bible on its binding and let it fall open. It opened to Psalm 52 and there on the page was my answer.

> Why do you glory in what is evil, you who are mighty by the mercy of God?

All day long

you are thinking up intrigues;

your tongue is like a sharpened razor,

you worker of deceit.

You love evil more than good,

lying rather than saying what is right.

You love all the words that create confusion,

you deceitful tongue.

God too will strike you down forever,

he will lay hold of you and pluck you from your tent,

uproot you from the land of the living.

The righteous will see and they will fear;

but they will laugh at him:

"Behold the man! He did not take God as his refuge,

but he trusted in the abundance of his wealth,

and grew powerful through his wickedness."

But I, like an olive tree flourishing in the house of God,

I trust in God's mercy forever and ever.

I will thank you forever

for what you have done.

I will put my hope in your name—for it is good,

—in the presence of those devoted to you.

(Psalms 52:3–11, NABRE)

The Psalmist's words were far worse than the punishment I had in mind, and it shook me up. From that point, I committed to praying daily for that person. The psalm so impacted me that I have a copy of it hanging in a can't-miss spot above my desk so that I'll never forget the lesson I learned the first time I read it. Whether a person is genuinely evil, mentally sick, or severely lacking good judgment, he or she is a child of God, and God will handle their transgressions as he sees fit. I have gone back to Psalm 52 many times, praying it through and giving my anger over to God. I have done this count-less times for my mother.

Pray for your mother, not only on the days she has upset you, but on every day. If you cannot bring yourself to pray for her directly, then pray for the desire to want to pray for her. Eventually, it will get easier. One day you will be able to pray for her with a sincere heart.

CHAPTER SIX

YOU'RE JUST LIKE YOUR MOTHER

Humility is the mother of many virtues because from it obedience, fear, reverence, patience, modesty, meekness and peace
are born. He who is humble easily obeys everyone, fears to
offend anyone, is at peace with everyone, is kind with all.[22]

—ST. THOMAS OF VILLANOVA

"You're just like your mother." The first time someone said that
to me, I was mortified. Being like my mother was the last thing I
wanted to be! In fact, I wanted to be as much unlike her as I possibly
could, and I vowed to make that a life goal. Try as I might, I could
not root all of Mom out of me. You will not be able to get all of your
mom out of you, either.

This morning, I used a fake, annoying voice and playfully woke
my college-age son with the line, "Get out of that bed, or I'll pull
you out!" He responded with a playful quip and we both laughed.
I was laughing for two reasons. First, at our kidding around with
each other. Second, because I heard my mother's voice coming out
of my mouth.

My mother often woke my dad or us kids that way; only her
annoying voice was menacing and not fake and playful. Her threat
was real and not kidding around. So how could I laugh about
hearing myself saying the same thing to my own son? I could

laugh—sincerely—because hearing my mother's voice come out of my mouth no longer shocks or disturbs me. Just because I imitate funny things my mother used to say does not mean that I am my mother. It just means that there are certain things we do similarly or characteristics that we have in common. I have accepted the parts of myself that are like my mother and have made them my own.

Please do not misunderstand. I did not say that I have become like my mother completely. I said that there are parts of me that are like parts of her. That is not the same thing. My mother and I have the same genes. That and the fact of having been raised by her makes it inevitable that some of my behaviors resemble some of hers. The key, however, is in realizing that and learning how to work with it with patience and God's grace.

This did not happen overnight, of course. It took me years to be able to stand back and laugh at both myself and the ridiculous things my mother did. Certainly, the things she did that are darkly abusive are not funny in any possible way, and I am not implying that. I am not implying that you should laugh at the things your mother did, either—at least not the ones that were truly hurtful or harmful. I am talking about the little moments when her childishness showed through in ways that can be sloughed off as quirks in her behavior. I am also talking about the little moments when those quirks show through in our own behavior.

It probably has happened for you already. If not, it most likely will—not just once but many times. And that is okay, as long as you deal with it appropriately. For me, dealing with the instances in which I acted, sounded, or reacted like my mother required me to make a choice as to how I would respond to the situation. If what I found myself doing or saying was just silly or harmless, I admitted it was silly or harmless, brushed it off, and let it go. If it was harmful, I admitted that it was harmful and resolved to eradicate the behavior. Sometimes, it took many, many tries before I had rooted it out of my system. Other times, it was something for which I needed to seek help from a spiritual director, professional counselor, or both. Most importantly, I did not let it scare me. Granted, it did frighten me in the early years, but over time, I grew less afraid (a reactive response) and more proactive in the way I would handle such occurrences. How has this been possible? Because I had—and still have—access to God's grace. So do you.

Like it or not, you were born from your mother's womb. There is no way to ignore, refute, forget, or change that fact. Let's face it. If it were not for your mom, you would not even be here, and I am glad you are here. So are all the people in your life who love you. For that reason, I have to give your mom credit because she carried you in her womb and gave birth to you. I hope that you can find it in your heart to give her credit for that, too. The same holds true if you are dealing with a foster or adoptive mother.

Along these lines, I think there are two very important things for you to keep in mind—two things that it took me some time to come to grips with in myself. First, because you were born from your mother, you are genetically predestined to particular traits and, to a degree, particular behaviors. You are also prone to share similarities with the mother who raised you if she was not your birth mom. Second, you are a separate being from your mother and have the option and ability to behave differently from her and cultivate traits that are unlike hers. What's more, you have the possibility of exhibiting the same traits and behaviors in a completely new and grace-filled way.

Let me give you an example. I do not wear any jewelry except for the medal that signifies the Covenant of Love I made with the Blessed Mother through the Schoenstatt Movement. This is a conscious decision I made years ago and is an aesthetical practice of sorts. You see, my mother was obsessed with fine jewelry, constantly buying and trading in pieces for new, more extravagant ones even though our family budget could not afford it. Sometimes, she would even spend extravagantly on me and then demand that I wear the pieces or face her wrath. As an adult, I felt an urgent call to forsake jewelry. Firstly, it was a marked statement of dissimilarity between my mother and myself. I never, ever, wanted to get caught in that trap of obsession as Mom had been. Secondly, I wanted to make up for the sins of my mother by sacrificing the very thing that had been a source of pain for our family as well as an offense against the Sacred Heart of Jesus and the Immaculate Heart of Mary. The only time I wear jewelry is when it is done at a special occasion in honor of my children, such as on their wedding days. Elsewise, I remain purposefully unadorned. This has been a meaningful and spiritually edifying resolution for me, and I have experienced countless graces because of it.

God's grace can and will do that for you if you are open to it. In his work *Summa Theologica*, St. Thomas Aquinas wrote about the effects of grace on the human mind and heart: "Since therefore grace does not destroy nature but perfects it, natural reason should minister to faith as the natural bent of the will ministers to charity."[23] In other words, through grace, what we have been given at birth becomes refined and holy.

After I had written my first book, I was told by my publisher that in order for it to sell well, I would have to get on the public speaking circuit. Being a very shy person, that was the last thing I wanted to do! On the other hand, I wanted my book to be successful. So, I took a deep breath and jumped into the pool, figuratively speaking. When I look back, I realize that I was able to that because of one of the gifts I had been given by my mother—gumption. My mother's gumption could at times be her worst enemy and at other times her greatest advantage. Her gumption is what gave her the spunk and determination to survive a traumatic childhood and a tough adult life. It also drove her to be combative and insulting to others who crossed her path, including her own husband and children. I inherited Mom's gumption and had the choice to allow it to become an advantage or drive me to be oppositional and abrasive like she was. I chose the former and with God's grace I was able to cultivate the gumption to work in my favor.

St. Germaine Cousin is a wonderful example of grace perfecting nature. She was born in Pibrac, France, in 1579 with a crippled right arm and later developed an unsightly, purulent disease called "scrofula." The disease caused boil-like sores to grow around her neck and on her cheek, affected her bones and joints, and caused open and running abscesses. Her origins are unclear. She may have been abandoned at the door of Laurent Cousin or may have been the child of his first wife who had died in the plague. Either way, she ended up in the custody of Laurent and his second wife, Armande, on the Cousinses' family farm during a time of severe poverty and unrest in France.

Armande came to live at the Cousinses' farm when Germaine was four or five years old, and she hated the little girl from the start. Whether it was because Germaine was not her own child, because some of her own children had died shortly after birth, because Germaine was physically deformed, or a combination of all those factors, is a mystery. For whatever reason, Armande abused Germaine terribly, forcing her to live in the barn and sleep on a bed of straw and twigs. Germaine was never allowed into the house and was fed only a piece of stale bread or the meager table scraps left-over from Armande's other children. She was made responsible for tending the sheep, herding them shoeless in the heat of summer and brutal cold of winter near a forest infested with vicious wolves. On top of that, she was required to spin a certain amount of wool every day—despite her disabilities—or face punishment if she failed. She was deprived of an education, beaten, publicly humili-ated, and falsely accused by Armande. Once, she scalded Germaine by pouring boiling water over her legs. Nothing, it seemed, could prevent the stepmother's wrath.

Surprisingly, however, Germaine was allowed to attend Mass in the village church, St. Mary Magdalen, on the other side of the river. Attending Mass gave her great joy amid her sorrowful life. She participated with ardor and eagerly absorbed the catechism lessons for children that took place afterward. Through the Mass, Germaine found meaning and strength in her suffering, and she began to see her life as a mission of love. She united her suffering with that of the Savior's and offered it for others, including the conversion of her stepmother.

Eventually, Sunday Mass was no longer enough for Germaine, and she yearned to attend daily Mass. But what would she do with her flock? One day she decided to try an experiment. She gathered her sheep together and stuck her spindle in the middle of them, praying that they would remain there while she was at Mass. She returned from the church to find the sheep still there, perfectly safe.

This was the first of many such miracles attributed to Germaine, including the parting of the flooded river in order for her to pass on her way to the church, and the appearance of flowers in her bundled apron when accused by Armande of having stolen bread from the kitchen to feed a beggar. As her holiness grew, so did her popularity among the village children. They sought her company and loved to listen to her speak about the faith and pray the rosary with them. As Germaine's reputation grew, Armande's hatred and abuse of her grew as well. Yet, the girl never showed her stepmother anything but love and obedience. Initially, the people of Pibrac believed Armande's wild stories about Germaine's wickedness and scoffed at her, calling her "The Devout One." After witnessing the children's love for her and seeing for themselves Germaine's endless humility and patience, they began to call her "The Devout One" with admiration and affection instead of disdain.

For unknown reasons, Laurent did nothing about his daughter's abuse for the first twenty years of her life. Then suddenly, he had a change of heart and demanded that she be allowed her rightful place among the family's other children, living in the house and being cared for properly. Armande, too, began to experience a change of heart. Nonetheless, Germaine insisted on continuing her life of suffering and poverty for Jesus and the sake of others. Two years later, the little shepherdess's body succumbed to the disease, and she died in her sleep on her bed of straw in the barn. She was buried in the village church, and many more miracles have been attributed to her since her death, including the fact that her body remains incorrupt to this day. She was canonized by Blessed Pope Pius IX in 1853.

I cried when I first read the story of St. Germaine, and I still get choked up when I think about this little saint. I saw myself in her, and many of the abuses she suffered are ones that I suffered, too. I also saw shadows of my own mother in her stepmother, Armande, and share with St. Germaine similar reactions of the people around me to my mother's false accusations. I have a lot in common with St. Germaine, and I can imagine that you do, also. It was not easy for me to read the details of her life, nor was it easy to relay them here for you to read. I did it not to dredge up painful memories for you or sensationalize abuse. Rather, I included St. Germaine's story in full in this chapter so that you can see how nature was perfected by grace. St. Germaine's devotion to our Lord in the Eucharist and his Blessed Mother in the rosary transformed her from being a derided and unwanted victim to becoming a loved, loving, and joyful saint.

This is precisely the reason why you can and will be able to hear people say, "You're just like your mother," and not fall to pieces or get angry. It is the reason why you can and will be able to hear your mother's voice come out of your mouth and chuckle to yourself. You are no longer a derided, unwanted, abused victim. You can share traits with your mother and exhibit behaviors similar to hers without feeling threatened that you either already are or will become like her. If you turn yourself over to Jesus and seek him frequently in the Eucharist, he will strengthen and uphold you. If you allow his grace into your heart, it will begin to transform you. Likewise, if you seek Mary's companionship and intercession as St. Germaine did, you will find peace and consolation in the folds of her mantle.

St. Germaine loved to pray the rosary because through it, she was drawn closer to our Lord and his Mother. The rosary is not some bizarre form of Mary worship. It is an age-old custom of prayer that takes us, one decade at a time, deeper into the lives of

Jesus and Mary. It is a common misconception that the rosary is only about Mary; it is actually more about Jesus. Beginning with the Joyful Mysteries and on through the Glorious Mysteries, the rosary traces the life of Christ from conception to death and resurrection. The rosary is a descendant of the ancient practice of monks to use pebbles, sticks, or lines drawn in the sand to count their prayers as they said them. At the time, it was part of their discipline to say a series of seventy-two Our Fathers—not easy to count on one's fingers! Eventually, the Hebrew practice of praying 150 psalms was adopted and adapted by Christians in monasteries and knotted cords took the place of pebbles and sticks.[24] In 1214, the Blessed Virgin Mary appeared to St. Dominic and instructed him in the method we know as the rosary today—five sets of ten Hail Marys with beads in between representing Our Fathers and Glory Bes. It became a tool for countering the heresy of the Albigensians and for teaching and remembering the chief truths of our Catholic faith.[25]

I, like St. Germaine, find great consolation in saying the rosary. I learned it as a child in Catholic grade school, and it grew in me over time. It was my weapon of choice, so to speak, whenever my mother's hostility toward me would start escalating. If I could, I would escape the situation physically and go somewhere I could pray undisturbed. If I could not escape, I would say it slowly and purposefully in my mind. Mentally, it transported me to another place where I was safe from my mother's wrath. Of course, I tried never to let on to my mother what I was doing! She did catch me a few times, huddled in my room with the rosary in my hands. It only served to irritate her more and elicited another round of verbal abuse. I got the same kind of treatment for attending Mass. Yet she never stopped me. Strangely, my mother had strong respect for holy things—priests, nuns, churches, and sacramentals like rosaries. To her dying day, she slept with a rosary every single night. I have no idea whether or not she prayed it, but her set of beads was always with her at night. I have done the same myself for many, many years. I do not do it to directly imitate Mom, but rather because I like the calming effect it has on me. When I pray the rosary at night, I release all my cares and all who I worry about into the intercession of Mary. That, I think, is a great example of grace perfecting nature.

CHAPTER SEVEN

MOM! I NEED YOU!

Let them fly with utter confidence to this most sweet Mother of mercy and grace in all dangers, difficulties, needs, doubts and fears. Under her guidance, under her patronage, under her kindness and protection, nothing is to be feared; nothing is hopeless. Because, while bearing toward us a truly motherly affection and having in her care the work of our salvation, she is solicitous about the whole human race. And since she has been appointed by God to be the Queen of heaven and earth, and is exalted above all the choirs of angels and saints, and even stands at the right hand of her only-begotten Son, Jesus Christ our Lord, she presents our petitions in a most efficacious manner. What she asks, she obtains. Her pleas can never be unheard.[26]

—BLESSED POPE PIUS IX

It was in the wee hours of the sleepless night recently that I came upon this quote by Blessed Pope Pius IX. I could not sleep because I was wrestling with my worry over one of my own children and just could not turn my mind off. I tossed and turned, said multiple rosaries, tossed and turned some more, and said another rosary. Still restless and wide awake, I got out of bed, went downstairs, grabbed a book to read and sat down in our dining room where we've set up a prayer corner dedicated to the Blessed Virgin Mary.

I looked up at her picture, sighed, and said, "Mother, please. Give me a word or two. Anything. I need some direction."

I had initially picked up the book thinking that I would sit and read until I got sleepy, since I had already been saying rosaries for an hour and a half and had not been able to settle my mind down. After I spoke those words to Mary, I was inspired to pick up the book and open it to a random page. I closed my eyes and pulled open the book. I looked down at the page and there it was, staring me in the face—the quote from Blessed Pope Pius IX about Mary's ability to help in even the most seemingly hopeless situations.

Tears came to my eyes. I read the entire quote, slowly and out loud, two more times. Although written by Pius IX, each word seemed to have been sent directly to me from the Blessed Mother. I believe they were. Using the book as messenger, so to speak, she was sending me a message of consolation and hope and giving me direction with the difficulties I was facing. The words in the quote that stood out for me that night were "nothing is hopeless." No danger, difficulty, need, doubt, or fear is too much for Mary to handle.

One horrid night while I was living alone with my mother, she became ill. At least I think that is what was going on with her. She was in the bathroom and I suddenly heard her cursing wildly. Shortly after, she came out and ordered me to get into the bathroom and clean it up. I have never seen anything like what I saw in that room that night. I will save you the details, but suffice it to say that my mother must have been violently sick (mentally and physically) to create such a scene. I did not even know where to begin. The entire room would have to be scrubbed down and sanitized. I did not mind having to clean up after Mom—after all, if she was actually ill, she indeed needed help—as much as I minded the verbal abuse that continued to rain down on me as I did so. From her bedroom next door to the bathroom came a vicious, endless stream of expletives and insults. I have no idea what set off her aggression, and I certainly did not know how to stop it. So, I tried to ignore it. I grabbed a bucket, cleaner, and some rags and started scrubbing. The verbal slings were coming faster. Not knowing what else to do, I started to sing every Marian song I knew—loud, clear, and in an effort to drown out my mother's nastiness. I have to be honest, here. Part of the reason I chose Marian songs is because my devotion to Mary irritated my mother. I thought that perhaps she would stop berating me in order to get me to stop singing. Obviously, that did not work, because she just kept going.

Then something wonderful happened. As I sang, I felt peace and protection. The more I sang, the more peaceful and protected I felt. Before long, I was filled with an inexplicable sense of calm and joy that somehow lifted my heart up and out of that terrible situation and made me tangibly feel Mary's love and protection. I kept singing and cleaning, and Mom kept scolding me. When I was done, I put the cleaning supplies away and went to my own bedroom. Eventually, my mother quieted down. The ordeal was over.

I am not suggesting that you simply sing away your troubles with your mother; that would be superficial and unrealistic, unless, of course, singing does bring you peace and joy. But that is not what I am referring to in this instance. That night with my mother was for me a critical situation, and I started singing out of desperation so that I could keep my grip and drown out my mother's voice. I needed to mentally and emotionally remove myself from there and go to another place—someplace that had nothing to do with my mother or the mess I had before me. More importantly, it was a desperate reach for Mary and a plea for her to come to my rescue. I needed to feel close to her, right then and there. I could not go to her physically in the Marian Shrine as I wished I could, so I went to her musically and spiritually instead. It worked. By singing Marian songs, I was lifted out of the crisis and placed into the arms of the Blessed Virgin Mary—my mother and protector.

The inspiration to do this did not come from me, I guarantee you. It came from the Blessed Mother, and I am sure of that. I have no doubt that she invoked the Holy Spirit to inspire me to step out of that predicament, so to speak, and into her motherly care. She raced to my aid, enfolding me in her arms and helping me to feel secure in her love. What's more, that is not the only time that has happened to me; it has occurred repeatedly throughout my life. Mary has saved me many times from spiritual and physical danger. If it were not for her, I would not be here today writing this book!

Whenever I remember one of those times in which Mary rescued me from a serious predicament, I think of St. Thérèse of Lisieux. One of my favorite stories about her is when she was small and became so ill that her family assumed she was going to die. Thérèse's mother, Zelie Martin, had died of breast cancer when Thérèse was just four and a half years old.[27] Immediately, she adopted her older sister, Pauline, as a second mother.[28] When Thérèse was about nine years old, Pauline entered the Lisieux Carmel, a cloistered order of nuns, which meant the two would be permanently separated. This was more than Thérèse could bear, and in her grief, she came down with a severe and mysterious illness that caused constant headaches, trembling, fevers, and hallucinations. She wrote in her autobiography, "The sickness which overtook me certainly came from the demon; infuriated by [Pauline's] entrance into Carmel, he wanted to take revenge on me for the wrong our family was to do to him in the future."[29] With Pauline gone to cloister, Marie, the second oldest Martin daughter, was left to care for Thérèse. Bedridden, Thérèse continued to deteriorate into a condition the saint later described as an "inexplicable struggle." At the point that things seemed most dire, Thérèse's sisters Marie, Leonie, and Celine knelt at her bedside facing a statue of the Blessed Virgin Mary that rested on the dresser at the foot of the bed. Together, the girls prayed to Mary for a miracle.

Suddenly, the statue became radiant and Mary's face showed a kindness and tenderness, displaying a "ravishing smile" that penetrated deeply into Thérèse's soul. At that moment, she was cured. Moved to tears, Thérèse looked toward Marie and saw that she was looking back at her.

> Without any effort I lowered my eyes, and I saw Marie who was looking down at me lovingly; she seemed moved and appeared to surmise the favor the Blessed Virgin had given me."... "Yes, the little flower was going to be born again to life, and the luminous *Ray* that had warmed her again was not to stop its favors; the Ray did not act all at once, but sweetly and gently raised the little flower and strengthened her in such a way that five years later she was expanding on the fertile mountain of Carmel.[30]

The Little Flower was deathly sick, and the Blessed Mother simply reached out and saved her! I think that is an amazing story. Yet, when I first heard it, I thought to myself, *Of course Mary saved Thérèse. She's a saint!* Miracles always happen for saints. But here's the thing. Thérèse was not canonized until after her death. In other words, Mary did not save her because Thérèse was already a saint. Mary saved the Little Flower because she was a saint in the making. On May 13, 1883, in Les Buissonnets, France, Mary cured a little girl who loved her very much and whom she loved very much and saw as her own child. That child became St. Thérèse of Lisieux, named a Doctor of the Church in 1997 by St. Pope John Paul II.

You are a saint in the making as well. I am sure that might sound strange to you, but it is true. What's more, we all are saints in the making—some to more success, others to less success. That is what the Church teaches. Our Lord has called every single human being to holiness and requires us to strive for sanctity in our daily lives.

In the document from Vatican Council II, *Lumen Gentium*, (*People of Light*), the Church Fathers were absolutely clear in their declaration that holiness—and in that regard the striving for sanctity—is for everyone, not just a select few. "Fortified by so many and such powerful means of salvation, all the faithful, whatever their condition or state, are called by the Lord, each in his own way, to that perfect holiness, whereby the Father himself is perfect."[31]

That word *perfect* can cause us to cringe. When we hear it, we tend to think of someone who never, ever makes a mistake or commits any sin of any kind. That is not what is meant here. Further down in *Lumen Gentium*, the Fathers describe it quite beautifully.

> The followers of Christ are called by God, not because of their works, but according to His own purpose and grace. They are justified in the Lord Jesus, because in the baptism of faith they truly become sons of God and sharers in the divine nature. In this way they are really made holy. Then too, by God's gift, they must hold on to and complete in their lives this holiness they have received. They are warned by the Apostle to live "as

becomes saints," and to put on "as God's chosen ones, holy and beloved a heart of mercy, kindness, humility, meekness, patience," and to possess the fruit of the Spirit in holiness. Since truly we all offend in many things we all need God's mercies continually and we all must daily pray: "Forgive us our debts."[32]

This is what the canonized saints knew, and what you must know as well. Because you are God's child, you are a saint in the making. Also, because you are God's child, you are Mary's child. The two go hand in hand. Mary does not love you because you are a saint; she loves you whether or not you are a saint. She loves you even if you were the most wretched, hateful sinner to ever walk the earth! If you need help, she will help you. If you call out to her, she will come to your rescue. If you are ill, she will cure you. It may not happen in exactly the timing and manner in which you prefer, but it will happen. It will happen according to God's will for you through Mary's intercession and the love of our Lord Jesus Christ.

As long as you are Mary's child, she will always be at the ready to help you in any and every situation. St. Alphonsus Liguori was deeply in love with the Blessed Mother and wrote extensively about her. He had experienced her help in his own life and was certain that she would help others as well.

"Be of good heart, then, all you who are children of Mary. Remember that she accepts as her children all those who choose to be so. Rejoice! Why do you fear to be lost, when such a Mother defends and protects you?" he writes in his book, *The Glories of Mary.*[33]

"Be of good heart." I love that because it is true. We should be of good heart no matter what happens because we know—or we should know—that we are Mary's very own children and that she loves us beyond what words can adequately describe. We have, not only the right, but the obligation to call out to her when we are in trouble. Like all good mothers, her ears are tuned to the voices of her children. She knows each one individually and is constantly listening. It's like when a number of families are gathered in one place. Perhaps it's an event of some kind or even in the shopping mall. If one child gets hurt or lost and calls out to his mother, the mother hears his voice above all the others and knows immediately that it's her child's voice she hears. "Mom! I need you!" he calls out. She hears and rushes to his side. That is exactly the way it is with Mary, our heavenly Mother. No matter how many people there are in the world chattering away, yelling, shouting—or even singing— she knows each voice singularly. She hears the call, perceives the need, and rushes to her child's side. This sweet Mother of mercy and grace will be there for her children in all dangers, difficulties, needs, doubts, and fears. It is exactly as what Blessed Pope Pius IX said in the quote at the beginning of this chapter.

Mary knows your voice. She will hear your call, she will perceive your need, and then she will rush to your side. All you need to do is say, "Mom! I need you!" And she will be right there. Call her now. She is waiting to hear your voice above all the others.

Chapter Eight

Who Will Be a Mother to Me Now?

If you ever feel distressed during your day—call upon our Lady—just say this simple prayer: "Mary, Mother of Jesus, please be a mother to me now." I must admit—this prayer has never failed me.[34]

—St. Teresa of Calcutta

After I moved out of my mother's house, she tried hard to pull me back in, to get me to move back home, or at least back to the same city as she was in. I continued to have contact and visit her, but I was determined to keep a safe distance between us. She tried lavish gifts, pleas for help—all kinds of things. I was not interested, and that upset her. When none of her efforts proved fruitful, she began harassing me by phone, calling at all different hours of the day and night. Sometimes she would speak when I answered, sometimes she would just hang up. When she did speak, it was initially sweet and then would get snarly. She would accuse me of various disgusting behaviors including, at one point, of being a prostitute! It was such a ridiculous notion that I laughed. What made it even more ridiculous is that I had decided to submit my application for the Schoenstatt Sisters of Mary that coming fall. I never told my mother that, lest it somehow backfire on me.

Not long after, I met a wonderful young man, realized that I had misperceived my vocation (that indeed is a story all its own), and we were married. Three years later, we had our first child and eventually three more plus one that we had lost to miscarriage. All throughout, I tried to keep contact with my mother and to visit on holidays or other occasions when I hoped it might be safe. That worked okay for a number of years, as I was able to act as a buffer between my mother's mentally ill behavior and my children. I'd field the rage-filled calls and grab the mail before the kids did so that I could sort it and remove the hate letters before anyone else laid eyes on them. Post-Christmas was always especially terrible, as there'd reliably be a hate letter sent that criticized me for what I'd written in the family Christmas letter. For some reason, those letters particularly drew her fire. Her criticisms were irrational and even incoherent but hurtful nonetheless. I stopped including letters in her cards, but her hate letters would still come, ridiculing the cards themselves. So, I stopped sending anything altogether. I backed off on personal and family visits to her as well.

As my children grew older, it became more difficult for me to be that buffer. Mom would call while I was out and try to fill the kids' heads with untrue stories and false accusations against me. She would scare them and warn them not to tell me about the conversation. Then came the letters addressed directly to my children. I let the first couple pass, thinking she might be trying to make amends and allowing the kids to open and read them on their own. I wanted them to have a relationship with both of their grandmothers (my mother-in-law is a wonderful grandmother!), and I also wanted to teach them respect for older generations. But I started sensing a change in my mother's tone and could see the angry slant in her handwriting. I knew Mom's penmanship well. When the writing changed, I started insisting that I be the only one to get the day's mail. I would sift out the letters from Mom to the kids before anyone else saw them. She especially targeted my daughter—I have never figured out why. Perhaps it was because I was not the daughter she wanted me to be for her. Regardless, the final straw came when a particularly nasty letter arrived for my daughter. I could see there was no hope. I discussed it with my spiritual director, and we both agreed that the time had come to cut off contact completely. I still can see his face and hear his words.

"You have no choice. You must do this to protect your family and yourself. You do not owe your mother contact because of the way she treats you."

After that, all correspondence from Mom was straight away torn up and thrown in the trash. I accepted calls from her, but mostly because this was before the days of caller ID, so I never knew who would be on the other end of the line when I picked up. Since I have always worked out of my home, our home phone was also my work phone, so I needed to answer calls. When my mother and I did connect by phone, I kept it superficial and brief. I gave her little or no information about myself or my family and let her do all the talking about herself and her own life. Gradually, the space between the calls became greater and then stopped entirely. It was very hard for me to face my children's questions. They would ask why we were not visiting Grandma anymore, and I would always answer, "Grandma is sick." I had no other way to explain it to them. I did not want them to judge their grandmother, nor did I want them to judge me. Additionally, I wanted to leave the door open in the case that my mother would someday change. I was not happy with the separation from my mother, but there simply was no other option. Years earlier, I had suggested she seek counseling, and she became aggressively hysterical. So I never brought it up again for fear I would get the same or worse reaction from her. It did not seem likely that Mom would ever change, and consequently, the separation would have to continue.

One day, our oldest child became frustrated with always receiving the same reason for our distance from my mother. "If Grandma is so sick that we can't see her, then why don't you go help her?" he demanded. I tried very hard to give a proper explanation that would satisfy my son and still protect my mother's reputation. Most of all, I wanted to protect my children's innocence—I felt this issue was far too complex for their young hearts and minds. Afterward, I felt so horrible that I went upstairs to my bedroom and had a long, long cry.

In my heart of hearts, I knew my son was right. If Mom was so sick, why wasn't I helping her? Absolutely, reinitiating contact was not an option. Not, at least, until God gave me a definitive indication that my mother had indeed changed. I did a great deal of praying and soul-searching. Finally, it became clear to me. I did need to help my mother, but I needed to do it spiritually, not actually. I waited for a quiet time (tough to come by when you've got a house with four home-schooled, preteen kids!), and I had a long talk with the Blessed Mother. The conversation is too personal to share word-for-word, but basically, I poured my heart out to her. I cried, complained, and ranted about all the pain I had suffered, all the fears I had harbored, and all the wishes and dreams I had held on to. Then, I surrendered my mother to Mary, asking her to take charge of Mom in all the ways that I could not. I also pledged to pray for my mom every single day with intent and sincerity. I had been praying for Mom before then, but mostly on the occasions she hurt or irritated me. From that day forward, I would pray for her no matter what. With that, I let go of my mother and put her into Mary's care. Once I did that, I felt a huge release of emotion followed by an overwhelming peacefulness.

It was then as well that I realized how truly and completely Mary had been my mother since my childhood and throughout my whole life. I thought again to the occasion when I was just a year old and the chance meeting that took place between my mother and Fr. Kentenich. I pondered the moment Fr. Kentenich held me and consecrated me to the Blessed Virgin Mary. From then on, Mary had been my mother in every possible way. When Fr. Kentenich consecrated me, he put me into the care of the Blessed Mother, as I had just done for my own mother.

In studying Fr. Kentenich's life, I see that he could do this for me because it had been done for him. When Fr. Kentenich's mother, Katharina Kentenich, was twenty-one, she was employed as kitchen help on an estate in the North Rhine-Westphalia area of Germany. Employed at the same farm as administrator was Matthias Koep, who was twenty-two years her senior. He took great interest in the hardworking, lively, and vivacious Katharina. Katharina was a deeply devout Catholic woman, and Matthias was described as a pious, upright, and honorable man who also was a devout Catholic. They entered into a relationship, and it seems that he promised to marry her. Then Katharina became pregnant, and romance turned to scandal. The expectation of the times was that the father of the child would marry the mother. But, for indefinite reasons, Matthias refused. Speculation is that the age difference troubled him, that he was a confirmed bachelor and did not want to give up his independence, or that his sense of integrity and honor caused him to be horrified by his sexual sin and thus stopped him from marrying Katharina. No one knows for certain, but what is certain is that there was little contact between Katharina and Matthias after that and later-life attempts on the part of Katharina or Joseph to have contact were unsuccessful. In fact, Matthias and Joseph never personally met, and Matthias never acknowledged Joseph as his son—to Joseph nor anyone else—and never mentioned him publicly.[35]

This left Katharina in a terrible predicament. Not only did she have to bear public shame, but her own parents initially rejected her. After a few months, they relented and allowed Katharina to move in with them. Katharina loved Joseph dearly and was committed to raising and providing for him herself, so after his birth, she continued to live with her parents and to work at various part-time jobs. Joseph's grandfather died when he was two-and-a-half years old, making Katharina's situation even more difficult as Matthias Kentenich (not to be confused with Matthias Koep—Joseph's father) had been the family's main source of income. Finally, Katharina procured a position as full-time cook for a wealthy family in Cologne. The problem was that such positions were open only to unmarried women, children were not allowed, and they were required to live on site. Joseph's grandmother Anna Maria was seventy-five, needed to work to support herself, and she was unable to care for the boy. What would become of Joseph?

Katharina's spiritual director, Fr. Savels, had a solution. The orphanage he had founded in 1882, St. Vincent's Orphanage, had an opening. Joseph could go there, where he would receive care and education under the administration of the Dominican Sisters. After struggling with the decision for nearly a year, Katharina finally decided to accept the priest's advice and place her son in the orphanage. Neither mother nor son welcomed the separation, but there was no other solution. On April 12, 1894, Katharina took her eight-year-old son and his belongings to the orphanage in Oberhausen, Germany. Before departing, Katharine took Joseph to the orphanage house chapel, where she knelt with him before a statue of Mary with Saints Dominic and Catherine of Sienna. Katharina took the only precious item she owned—her First Communion medal—and hung it around Mary's neck. She then consecrated her only child to the Blessed Mother and entrusted him to her care, praying, "Educate my child! Be entirely his Mother! Fulfill for me my duties as mother!"[36]

From early on, Joseph had shown an interest in the priesthood and exhibited a deep devotion to Mary. This moment of consecration and parting with his natural mother—Katharina—further impacted his relationship with his heavenly Mother—Mary. He did indeed become a priest, devoted his entire life to Mary, and went on to found the Apostolic Movement of Schoenstatt, a worldwide Catholic lay movement based on a Covenant of Love with the Blessed Mother.[37] But it was a long, tough journey. Katharina kept in touch with Joseph, and he visited her on school holidays, but the separation was brutal on his heart. Additionally, in those days, illegitimate children were banned from the priesthood. The only hope was to be exceptionally admitted to a religious order of priests. With Fr. Savels's help, Joseph was accepted into the Pallotine Fathers seminary. But his seminary years were tumultuous, and at one point he was nearly refused ordination. Finally, he was ordained a Pallotine Father in 1910.

After ordination, he was made spiritual director of the minor seminary and quickly won the love and admiration of the seminarians under his charge. This was during the turbulence of World War I, and Fr. Kentenich endured the hardships right along with the young men who were drafted into the military. Following behind were the frightening years of Hitler's reign and World War II, during which the Catholic Church was persecuted. The Schoenstatt movement, particularly its founder, was targeted, and consequently Fr. Kentenich spent four and a half years suffering degradation, starvation, beatings, and deprivation in the Dachau concentration camp. In 1954, he was exiled first to Switzerland and then to the United States as the Church tested—and later approved—the Schoenstatt Movement as a true work of God. Joseph Kentenich's life was filled with adversity, and yet he clung to Mary, his mother, throughout. In later years, he told his followers that he owed everything in his life to her.[38]

When he was fourteen years old, Joseph wrote a poem that he dedicated to his homeroom teacher in the minor seminary of the Pallotine Fathers. His teacher, Fr. Mayer, had taken Joseph under his wing, becoming his confidante and friend. The lines speak of Joseph's heartbreak over his separation from his mother and disownment by his father. It also reflects some of the struggles he faced in the seminary. I love this poem because I think it speaks to the worries and emotions that we face as children of troubled mothers. Although Joseph's mother was not troubled—she was a wonderful mother—he was separated from her, much as many of us are separated from our own mothers by circumstance or necessity.

THE POWER OF LOVE

You holy, noble, lofty band!

Which makes happy this our land!

Which relieves what weighs us down!

You holy, noble, lofty band!

You are the pledge of love!

Things otherwise impossible

Are possible for you, O Mighty One!

You would make yourself blind

If only others are happy

Through you! As fruits of your sacrifice,

Your constant struggle and your daring.

Evening spreads its wings

The sun, guided by Omnipotence,

Queen of the day, sinks

And sends nature the sign of peace.

Into the Western sea it bows!

Now darkness is around us—

Haste and bustle falls silent

Man rejoices in [night's] care!

An angel goes from door to door

To see if joy reigns here and there.

In order to console the downcast,

To gather the flowing tears.

Time processes: midnight comes,

The cathedral clock strikes 12 with might.

The sound of its toll spreads far,

Sounding forth along the Rhine.

It strikes midnight, and Cologne lies

In sweet silence, protected by the Lord
And Saints who watch o'er the great city;
Only the far corners are untouched.
A light casts out its shine
To the banks of Old Father Rhine,
Whose mirror is silver bright and clear;
Whose waves whisper well the truth.
And see! In this house is sitting
A boy! With head in hand,
Diligently learning,
Fighting sleep with all his might.
But dreamily he often looks afar
And whispers: O Lord, O God,
Guide my destiny.
I want to offer you my happiness
"Mine and my mother's too!
But no! Oh, no! It cannot be!
O Lord! I commend myself to you!
Let her relent, I beg of you!
"Preserve me from this step,
Hear, O Lord, the sinner's plea!
May you guide my mother's mind—
For I do not like to grieve her—
"That she may grant me my request,
To become a priest—Oh!—What?
But now everything in me pushes"
—He lets his tears flow freely—
"O God, not that! Not that, O God!
Let me rather die

Than not follow your call
And take up a career for which,
"O, Lord (I feel), you did not create me.
I hear, God, how you call me.
I want to follow you, though it's hard:
To love you, to increase your glory!
"From now on I want to fight
To dampen the resistance of my mother.
Grant me, O Lord, that it succeeds
So that your praise resounds.
"O Sea! You, the dream of my youth!
Should all my plans become mere foam?
I "want it"—trembling on your back—
Save my father, who is said to be sick
"But stop! I still have my duty."
The test tomorrow? It comes to mind
And reins in his thoughts
And he studies—until he falls asleep.
—J. Kentenich
To be continued![39]

The poem shows Joseph at study, preparing for a test the next day. Don't you and I find ourselves in like situations almost nightly? For those of us dealing with difficult moms, every next day is like a test. How do I deal with her? What mood will she be in? How do I avoid her wrath? What can I do to help her? All of these are like questions on a test—we must come up with the answers in order to survive. And for some of us, the test includes having to separate ourselves from our mothers for our own sake and that of our loved ones.

The great and consoling thing is that, like Fr. Kentenich, we have Mary as our real, constant, loving, and trustworthy Mother.

She never gave up on him, and she'll never give up on you or me. As a young boy, Fr. Kentenich was placed into Mary's care by his mother, but along with Katharina's consecration, he made one of his own, placing himself into Mary's care and asking her to become his Mother. I have no doubt that, at that moment, he also consecrated his natural mother and placed her into Mary's care. His confidence in the Blessed Virgin Mary was so profound that he spent his entire life leading others to her kind, motherly heart. For that reason, Fr. Kentenich is for me both example and hero.

Perhaps you have had to separate yourself from your mother, or she may have separated herself from you. Maybe you do not feel the need to separate at all or know you need to but have not gained strength enough to do it yet. Regardless, there is one single most important question for you to ask: Who will be a mother to me now?

The answer is Mary.

CHAPTER NINE

I FORGIVE YOU

He who knows how to forgive prepares for himself many graces from God. As often as I look upon the cross, so often will I forgive with all my heart.[40]

—ST. FAUSTINA

My spiritual director told me I would know when it was the right time to reconnect with my mother, and that time came after nearly twenty years of separation. My brother had randomly searched my mother's name on the Internet and discovered that a nearby Baptist church had posted in the weekly bulletin that she needed prayers. He searched further and discovered she had moved to a senior living center adjacent to the church. She had mentioned years before that she had gone to Sunday services at a Baptist Church in town; I thought she meant she had accompanied a friend out of curiosity—she had never been much of a churchgoer. But perhaps this was the same congregation and it had been more than a one-time visit. My brother contacted the facility and learned that, although her condition was stable, there were some definite health concerns. From what he could gather, members of the church had helped her to move out of her apartment and into the retirement home, and a lawyer from the congregation was appointed power of attorney over her finances and healthcare. My brother notified my sisters and me of his findings.

He felt strongly that we four siblings should reconnect with our mother, especially facing the reality that she was becoming aged and physically infirm. Regardless of how we have been treated, we owe a certain degree of respect to our parents in keeping with the fourth commandment, and I knew my brother was right in his thinking. He volunteered to call Mom, and when he did, they had a fairly civil conversation. He offered to take us all out to dinner at one of Mom's favorite restaurants. My oldest sister immediately refused, but my other sister was willing to fly in from her out-of-state home for the dinner. I was resistant to the idea—the mere thought of facing my mother again made me literally nauseous. I had reconciled with the past, healed a great deal from the memories, and was standing strong, so to speak, but I did not want to go back to the past. Even though I knew I was safe in the care of my spiritual mother Mary, I did not want to experience my natural mother's angst and aggression toward me or my children ever again. How could I be sure that would not happen when we met? I thought about it, prayed about it, talked to the Blessed Mother about it at length and switched my decision from no to yes and back again numerous times. Finally, I agreed.

On the day of the dinner, my brother and his two grown children plus my out-of-state sister visited with my mother at the retirement home before bringing her to the restaurant. My sister-in-law was scheduled to work that day and could not find a replacement. My sister and her husband had decided that he would not fly in with her, which was understandable. My husband, two younger sons, and I met them there. My oldest son and daughter declined the invitation, and I was not going to force them. It had been a difficult road with my mom, and I do not blame them for not wanting to come. They barely knew their grandmother, and what they did know was not very pleasant.

When we arrived at the restaurant, my sister met us at the entrance.

"I just wanted to warn you," she said. "Mom's in one of her moods."

I knew immediately what that meant and what was in store for us during the dinner.

"Oh, boy," I said.

"Yeah, it was pretty bad at the retirement home," she added.

She relayed some of what had happened—verbal abuse; foul-mouthed comments; wacky, mostly untrue stories with disgusting details; berating my dad and sister; and lots of lashing out. She had completely traumatized my niece to the point that the poor thing had to flee the room and wait down the hall. It was not a good situation. Things had not improved since they had gotten to the restaurant, my sister cautioned. I looked at my husband. He looked back at me. I knew what he was thinking.

"If you want to just turn around and go home, I'll take you," he said.

I took a deep breath and thought for a minute. My brother and his kids were there. My sister was there, and she had come all this way to join us. I simply could not just turn heel and dump the whole ugly situation in their lap, even though I knew they'd have understood.

"No," I answered my husband. "Let's go through with it."

"Okay," he assured me. "But remember, we can leave at any moment you say."

It was scary to see my mother again. She had aged consider-ably, but for the most part, she was the same woman she had always been, and her hardened, abrasive nature was as strong as ever, especially toward me. When she ended up in the seat directly across from me at our long, narrow table, I thought I would faint. Silently, I started repeating prayers for Mary's protection over and over and over. She glared at me and stiffened. I looked away and tried to hold conversation with the others.

It was extremely awkward, not just for me but for all of us. The rest of us made the best of it, talking, laughing, and joking around. Because of our upbringing, we siblings have learned to make the best of even the worst situations. We have become experts at glossing over my mother's public displays of crassness. I have to admit, it was really tough to do this that night at the restaurant. Mom was clearly uncomfortable—in spite of having agreed to come—and she slung insults left and right, particularly at the poor waitress who had no idea why she was being victimized. I felt terrible for her. My brother had ordered one of Mom's favorite dishes, but she barely touched it. My two sons sat to my right, and the high schooler kept the middle schooler engaged in conversation, distracting him from my mother's foul mouth and cruel affronts. Ignoring my attempts at conversing, Mom never said a word to me the entire meal. The only communication was her glaring eyes. When the meal was finally over, we said goodbye in front of the restaurant. I hugged everyone goodbye, including my mother, who responded by stiffening her body and giving me one last, hateful look. I did not regret the dinner and still am grateful to my brother for hosting it, but I knew then I would have to step back from Mom for the time being.

I actually have compassion toward my mother for her behavior that night. Imagine what it would be like to have been separated from your children for years—decades for some of us—and then suddenly be invited to dinner and surrounded by a number of them—and in a public establishment, to boot! Mom was out of her element, and her go-to response for such states of affairs was hostility. Because she had been abused and hurt so often in her life, her reflex was to lash out at others before they had a chance to lash out at her. Whether or not she understood why, we had hurt her, and she needed to hurt us before we hurt her again.

A couple of years after that dinner, we learned that Mom had been moved from the senior living facility to the advanced health-care facility. Her health had begun to decline. By this time, she was eighty-six years old. My husband and I had decided to make a pilgrimage to a Marian shrine a couple hours from our house, and the route took us directly past the city my mother was living in. On the way home, I made the daring decision to try again to connect with Mom. I am glad we did. She was completely different this time—pleasant, civil, docile, and grateful for our visit. The hate was gone, and for the first time in my life, I could make eye contact with my mother without a streak of terror running down my spine. Mom had indeed changed, I think in part because of her declining health and in part because dementia was taking hold of her mind. For whatever reason, I felt secure visiting with her and knew that the time had come to reconnect on a regular basis.

I visited my mother several times in the ensuing year and a half. Sometimes my husband or youngest son would accompany me, and sometimes I went alone. Each visit drove home further the realization that our roles had completely changed. It was as if I had become the mother and she had become the child. There was not a streak of meanness in her, and we were truly developing a relationship. We made small talk, and because of her failed memory, she would ask me questions, forget my answers, and ask the same questions again ten minutes later.

"So, how many rugrats have you got?" she would ask.

I would tell her the names and ages of each of my children.

"How's your sister? Is she still married to that bozo?" she would ask.

I would tell her about both of my sisters and their husbands.

Then she would ask about my brother and his family, and I would answer her questions yet another time.

We talked a lot about baseball, because Mom was an ardent, life-long fan. She still had the same transistor radio she had had when I was a kid, and she had it turned on 24-7. It was her only connection with the outside world. She'd get the players and announcers mixed up and wasn't too keen on the current win-loss record of her favorite team, but she never lost her enthusiasm for the game, and that radio was never turned off until the day she died.

I knew that my relationship with Mary had prepared me for this. I was strong enough and felt loved enough by the Blessed Mother to reach out to my natural mother. For forty-some years, I had prayed daily for the same intention: Before my mother died, let her change her ways and turn to God. She was certainly changing her ways; she was not ready to turn to God yet. On each visit, I could sense that she was further declining. Before long, she not only never left her room, but remained in bed. I offered countless times to take her around the retirement home or outside on the patio so she could get a change of scenery, but she adamantly refused.

I began to visit her more frequently, trying to get there at least bi-weekly and on holidays. Then one day, the nurse told me she had stopped eating. That is usually a sign that a person is preparing for death. I was desperately worried about the state of Mom's soul, and asked on every visit if we could pray the rosary together and if I could arrange for a priest to visit her, but she would have none of it.

"No," she would say. "I'm fine just the way I am."

I prayed to Mary and Fr. Kentenich, begging for their help. Their prayers had saved me; now I was asking them to save my mother. I had come to peace with my mother, and the only thing left was to get her back into God's arms before she passed away. But every visit garnered the same stubborn refusal. When it got to the point that Mom would go for days without eating, the nurse suggested that I bring in food to entice her. On the next trip, I brought hamburgers from McDonald's—two for her, two for me. We ate together, just the two of us, and Mom finished hers completely. In my memory, that was the only relaxed meal we had ever shared.

When I visited again, the nurse warned me that the end was nearing. I had been keeping my siblings informed of my visits and developments all along, so I shared this with them as well. My oldest sister still refused to have any contact with Mom, but my brother and his son visited a couple of times. Mom's second-shift nurse became a source of consolation and encouragement for me. She knew well Mom's volatile and abrasive character, and she had been estranged from her own mother for decades. She truly understood what my siblings and I were going through, and she kindly kept me up to speed on Mom's condition. The staff, she said, was quite surprised by our visits since Mom had never once mentioned that she even had children. She only told stories about her alcoholic husband who beat her all the time. That, of course, is fiction. We believe that, in her frail-mindedness, she must have been confusing her father with her husband. The nurse agreed to summon me when the end was near. The home's social worker also became an advocate for us, acting as the mediator between us and the attorney. She obtained permission for our visits and was able to give us some information about Mom's status and state of affairs. When I could not visit personally, I could check up on my mother via the social worker.

I got the call on June 15, 2015, sometime around nine in the morning. It was the social worker, calling to offer her condolences over the loss of my mother. She felt terrible when she realized I had not been informed of Mom's passing in the night. Apparently, the attorney had not added me to the list of people to be notified when my mother entered her final hours. I had so very much wanted to be with her during that time, if not to pray with her, then definitely to pray for her as she faced her Savior. Now she was dead, and there was nothing I could do to change that. The social worker assured me that Mom had died peacefully in her sleep—the aides had found her passed away at about 2 AM.

"Did the priest administer Last Rites before she died?" I asked.

"I'm sorry. I don't think so, but I don't know for sure," she responded. "But I will find out for you, I promise."

"Can I come to say goodbye to her body?" I asked.

"I'm sorry," the social worker said. "It's already gone. They took it away hours ago. Your mother had donated her body to the medical college for research, and so it was given directly to them."

The medical college was ninety minutes from my home. There was no way I would be able to get permission from the attorney and make it to the college before Mom's body became property of the college. Mom had threatened many times to donate her body to science, but we thought she was being overly dramatic and seeking attention. Turns out that she meant it. Whether done out of heart-break or cruelty, she planned to deprive us of the possibility of a last farewell.

I thanked the social worker on behalf of my siblings and myself and asked her to extend our gratitude to the rest of the staff. I hung up the phone and sat silently at my desk. Suddenly, I started to tremble from head to toe. It was mix of emotions at the prospect of having the years of abuse end permanently and also mortification at the thought that Mom had died without the opportunity to receive the sacraments before she died. What would happen to her soul? Yes, she was a vixen, and yes, I had many emotional scars from her mistreatment. Still, I did not want her to go to hell. I do not want anybody, ever, to go to hell. That made my heart terribly heavy.

I emailed my siblings the news, laying out all the details I knew. Then I sent text messages to my husband and children. I did not make any phone calls; I just did not want to talk to anyone right then. Rounds of emails and texts followed, everyone trying to grasp the situation and its impact. The weirdest thing is that there was… nothing. No estate to close, no funeral to plan, no coffin to choose, no grave to secure. Just empty space. The couple of days following were quiet as well. Hardly anyone we siblings knew also knew my mom, and the people who did know her did not know us. There was a solemn feeling of incompleteness—my siblings and I needed closure.

My out-of-state sister suggested that we have a memorial Mass for Mom, for her sake and our own. That was the perfect solu-tion! My brother and I agreed on the spot. My oldest sister backed off entirely. She did not want anything to do with Mom while she was alive and less once she had passed away. So the three of us remaining siblings worked on the Mass—choosing the date, place, and time, and we put together the Liturgy. The Schoenstatt Sisters of Mary generously offered the chapel of their Provincial House for the Mass and their retreat center dining hall for a meal afterward. A dear Schoenstatt Father-friend agreed to celebrate the Mass, two close musician-friends agreed to do the music, and four other close friends agreed to do the Offertory Procession.

Two days after Mom had died, I received another call from the retirement home social worker. She could not wait to tell me the wonderful news—my mother had indeed received last rites before she passed away! As I held the phone to my ear, I could feel the tears welling in my eyes. On Memorial Day, the Catholic priest from the nearby parish had visited my mother and, with her agreement, administered the sacraments. There is absolutely no description for the total joy and gratitude I experienced at that moment. No one can judge another person's soul, but I knew—according to the Church's teaching—that receiving last rites opens the possibility of heaven regardless of what kind of life the person has led. The door had been opened for Mom. The three things I'd begged God for over decades were given to me: That she'd come to peace with herself and with us kids, that she'd die peacefully and without suffering, and that she would return to the Church before death. All three of my petitions had been granted.

I think I can speak for my siblings in that, as we worked on the Mass, we felt a great burdensome weight being lifted from our shoulders. Years of emotional, spiritual, and relational hardship gently eased, and as the Mass got closer, our excitement grew. My husband, a printer, made booklets for the liturgy and memorial cards for the guests. One of my daughters-in-law worked with my youngest son to put together a display table with decorations and pictures (what happy ones we could find) of my mother. Even amid the strange circumstances, this was a blessed time for all of us.

The Mass itself was incredibly beautiful and grace-filled. A decent-sized handful of friends came. My brother, his wife, and his son were there, as well as my out-of-state sister and her husband. It meant a great deal to me to have my husband, children, daughters-in-law, granddaughter, and even the young man my daughter soon would marry present. I had given them all their choice whether or not to come. I believe they came primarily to support me rather than for the grandmother they barely knew, and it meant the world to me. It felt good to have everyone present, and we dearly missed my oldest sister. She had declined to have anything to do with the memorial Mass for mom, and to this day, she does not want to hear anything about it. I am very sad for her because I think she missed an important opportunity for healing and closure. But she had a right to and a reason for her decision, and we all accept that.

When we were planning the Mass, Father had requested that one of us siblings give a short speech of remembrance just before the liturgy started. My siblings nominated me—not my personal choice, but I agreed to their wishes. In preparing the text, I kept thinking back to some advice a friend had given me when I lamented that there would be no funeral or burial for my mother.

"Yes, there's no body," she said. "But that's just the body. It is her soul that matters. The soul is not the body!"

Those wise, comforting words rang in my head over and over and helped me to craft my words of remembrance. I would like to share with you what I said, partly to finish my own story and partly so that it can perhaps influence your own story. Read on and you will understand.

Words of Remembrance

Eva May Steinhage Memorial Mass, June 25, 2015

My friend Maria said it best. When I told her about my mother's death and memorial arrangements, she said, "The body is not the soul. It's the soul that matters."

Since we spoke, I have been mulling over her words.

The body is not the soul. It is the soul that matters.

This applies in many ways to our mother. The body is not the soul. It is the soul that matters.

Mom suffered a great deal during her lifetime, and consequently, her suffering affected those close to her.

But because the body is not the soul, whatever torment my mother had to endure has passed away along with her body, and her soul is free to seek union with God.

In the months before her death, I tried to arrange for her to receive the last rites, but my efforts met with obstacles.

Two days after her death, I learned that she had indeed been anointed—on Memorial Day, a holiday that was dear to my dad's heart. How perfect is that?

In our Catholic faith, we believe that the sacrament of anointing of the sick, or last rites, gives the dying courage and peace, union with Christ, forgiveness of sin, and preparation for the final journey.

My mother was able to receive this, and I saw it in her eyes during my last visit with her.

During my previous visits, I sensed that she had come to peace with herself and with the world.

On my last visit with her—two days before she died—I noticed a huge change in her, which at the time I took to be weakness.

Before I left, I told her, "See you soon, Mom." She did not respond.

Now I know why: her demeanor was not weakness, but rather resignation and readiness. She knew it was time. She was ready to go.

The body is not the soul. It is the soul that matters. Our mother is now free of all that hindered her during her lifetime.

This is precisely why my siblings and I decided that the theme for this memorial Mass should be hope and gratitude.

We have hope in the resurrection of Christ and that Mom will be welcomed into heaven to be with our Lord for eternity, and we have gratitude for the fact that it was through her womb that God chose to bring us to life.

The priest commended my mother's soul to God on Memorial Day. Now it is time for us to look to the future with hope and joy and to take with us the gifts that have been given to us through our mother's life.

The first gift is the gift of life itself. Without our mother, we would not have our spouses, children, nieces and nephews, grand-children, extended family, friends, talents, or personalities. Indeed, we would not be here to appreciate all that is beautiful and mean-ingful to us. Life.

Second, we have our mother to thank for our propensity toward service. From correcting papers for the teachers at St. Philip Neri, to volunteering to help with the parish Catholic Youth Organization, to joining a citizen action group to assist the police during the 1967 Milwaukee race riots, to organizing Christmas parties for orphans, she showed us how to serve the Church and community. Service.

Third, we have our mother to thank for our determination, which in some circles would be considered pig-headedness. The upside is that we are not easily put off, nor do we easily give up. Determination.

Fourth, we have our mother to thank for our gumption. One of our mother's most frequently used sayings is, "I don't take nothin' from nobody." We siblings, and now the next generation, have fine-tuned that gruffness into initiative, spunk, and resourcefulness. Gumption.

Fifth, we have our mother to thank for our drive to survive. Mom has always been a survivor, making it through a tough childhood and a tough life. After my dad's death, she managed to care for herself until the age of eighty-six. We siblings and now our children have inherited that drive to survive.

Sixth, we have our mother to thank for the gift of laughter. From her, we inherited the ability to laugh at ourselves. It is a unique gift, one that keeps us from taking ourselves too seriously and one that I know we have all found to be handy in awkward situations. Laughter.

These are six nameable gifts; I have no doubt others will surface as time goes on.

Like the many gifts we have received from our father, we will experience the gifts from our mother unexpectedly popping up here and there. And we will give thanks.

Regardless of what has been said or not said, done or not done, we have reason for hope and gratitude because we have been given much through God's grace.

We can let go now of our mother's body and release her soul to God's care.

Because the body is not the soul.

Forgiveness, they say, it a decision and not a feeling. I believe that's true. I would also add that forgiveness is a process, in that there is much work to be done once the decision to forgive has been made. For me, the decision to forgive was made when I was still quite young. It was not so much that I wanted or felt I needed to forgive Mom, but rather that I knew I should forgive her. The process began in earnest once I had grown into adulthood and especially when my husband and I started a family of our own. It accelerated once I had distanced myself from my mother and skyrocketed when I resumed contact by visiting her at the retirement home. It was completed during the memorial Mass my siblings and I had for her.

It hit me during Holy Communion. My siblings, I, and our families received the Eucharist first. Then the others in attendance lined up. I was praying silently and our friends were singing the Communion hymn "I Am the Bread of Life." The entire song dug deep into my heart, but the refrain was what really got me:

> And I will raise you up,
> And I will raise you up,
> And I will raise you up on the last day.

I was suddenly profoundly aware that the dead are not the only ones to be raised up. Those of us who cling to hope, who rely on God's grace and remain faithful to him are raised up above the trials, suffering, persecution, confusion, and helplessness of this life. My mother, my siblings, and I had been raised up. It was over. There would be no more vulgar insults, hateful glares, lies, wicked deceptions, taunting, betrayal, or fear ever again. God had seen me through with his goodness and mercy and eased my way by giving me a spiritual Mother to love and guide me. No matter what, my mother could never hurt me again. She would never, ever hurt herself or anyone else again. My mother was free and so was I.

I bowed my head and sobbed. During all those years with my mother, I had never allowed myself to cry at what she had done to me, because of me, or around me. Stubbornly, I refused to give her the satisfaction of my tears. I could not afford to show any weakness because she would take advantage of it. But then, sitting in the pew at Mom's memorial Mass, I cried. I suspect that our guests thought I was crying with sadness over my mother's death. To a point, yes. I was crying with pity over a life robbed of its innocence by abuse— hers as well as mine. Mainly, though, I was crying with relief. It finally was all over. My siblings and I were free of the hostilities, atrocities, and traumas inflicted on us by our mother, and she was free of the torment and desperation that had plagued her all of her life. Relief. Gratitude. Joy. Hope. Those are the tears that I shed that day, and at that moment, the decision and process of forgiveness had come to an end. I had forgiven Mom and let go.

I want that for you. God wants it for you, and your heavenly Mother wants it for you, too. Whether your mom is alive, ailing, or long gone, I want you to feel the peace, forgiveness, and hope that I feel. Just as it was for me, it will be a decision and a process for you. But the process will not be complete until it has begun.

I am going to ask you to do a daring thing right now. It might even seem like a silly thing to do. But please do it. You will not regret it, I promise. Sit back—regardless of where you are—and take a deep breath. Close your eyes and picture Mother Mary. There is no right or wrong way to picture her; let your mind conjure up an image of her that seems beautiful and inviting. Speak to her. Ask her to place her hands on your shoulders and guide you. Then imagine Mary standing behind you, gently resting her hands on your shoulders, and wearing a lovely smile. If you can, feel the subtle weight of her hands and the nearness of her love. Allow your heart to hope—for a deeper relationship with Mary and for the strength and courage to forgive and let go of the pain your natural mother has caused you.

Remember the sensation of that moment and go back to it as often as you wrestle with feelings of resentment, anger, or fear toward your mom. Whether that is once a month or once an hour, Mary will be there for you. She will never tire of resting her holy hands on your burdened shoulders. What is more, she will never tire of guiding you toward forgiveness because she knows that her son requires it of you. You must forgive, as must I, as must every follower of Christ.

There are three Scripture passages about forgiveness that I refer to when I am struggling to forgive. I find them to be a great help to me in getting my mind and heart ordered and receptive.

The first is from the Gospel of Matthew, and it is the scene in which Jesus teaches the Our Father to his disciples.

> This is how you are to pray:
> Our Father in heaven,
> hallowed be your name,
> your kingdom come,
> your will be done,
> on earth as in heaven.
> Give us today our daily bread;
> and forgive us our debts,
> as we forgive our debtors;
> and do not subject us to the final test,
> but deliver us from the evil one.
>
> If you forgive others their transgressions, your heavenly Father will forgive you. But if you do not forgive others, neither will your Father forgive your transgressions." (Matthew 6:9–15, NABRE)

"Forgive us our trespasses as we forgive those who trespass against us." Our Lord says directly that we will not be forgiven our own sins if we don't forgive the sins of others. That includes everyone, including your mother. Whenever you're tempted to retaliate for your mother's hurtful or sick behavior, say the Our Father slowly and deliberately as many times as it takes for you to calm down and are able to think and act in a rational and godly way.

The second Scripture passage I rely on for forgiving is from John's First Letter.

> What was from the beginning,
> what we have heard,
> what we have seen with our eyes,
> what we looked upon
> and touched with our hands
> concerns the Word of life—
> for the life was made visible;
> we have seen it and testify to it
> and proclaim to you the eternal life
> that was with the Father and was made visible to us—
> what we have seen and heard
> we proclaim now to you,
> so that you too may have fellowship with us;
> for our fellowship is with the Father
> and with his Son, Jesus Christ.
>
> We are writing this so that our joy may be complete.
>
> God is Light.
>
> Now this is the message that we have heard from him and proclaim to you: God is light, and in him there is no darkness at all.

If we say, "We have fellowship with him," while we continue to walk in darkness, we lie and do not act in truth.

But if we walk in the light as he is in the light, then we have fellowship with one another, and the blood of his Son Jesus cleanses us from all sin.

If we say, "We are without sin," we deceive ourselves, and the truth is not in us.

If we acknowledge our sins, he is faithful and just and will forgive our sins and cleanse us from every wrongdoing. (1 John 1:1–9, NABRE)

"God is light, and in him there is no darkness at all.... If we walk in the light as he is in the light, then we have fellowship with one another and the blood of his Son Jesus cleanses us from all sin."

For someone who has a troubled mother, it's easy to get sucked into the darkness. Be it from mental or spiritual illness or outright sinfulness, our mothers are trapped in a kind of darkness that may be keeping them from walking in Christ's light. If we stay close to Jesus and his mother—our mother—our own sins will be forgiven, and we'll be able to forgive our mothers' sins.

Third is a passage from the Gospel of Mark.

Jesus said to them in reply, "Have faith in God."

Amen, I say to you, whoever says to this mountain, "Be lifted up and thrown into the sea," and does not doubt in his heart but believes that what he says will happen, it shall be done for him.

Therefore I tell you, all that you ask for in prayer, believe that you will receive it and it shall be yours.

When you stand to pray, forgive anyone against whom you have a grievance, so that your heavenly Father may in turn forgive you your transgressions. (Mark 11:22–25, NABRE)

"When you stand and pray, forgive anyone against whom you have a grievance."

Jesus calls us to take to prayer all of the grievances we have against our mothers. He doesn't tell us to dismiss or downplay them. He doesn't tell us we have no right to them; he tells us to go to him and reckon with them prayerfully. He is asking us to have faith in him to deal with our mothers in justice and mercy. And he will—in his time and in his way.

That's easier to write or to say than it is to live. I know. How can you forgive someone who hurts you over and over again? You may not want to forgive your mom, but you must. So the first step in the forgiveness process is to ask for the grace to want to forgive. Take it to prayer. Ask Jesus, "Lord, grant me the grace to want to forgive." Once you begin to feel the desire, ask him, "Lord, I want to forgive, please help my unforgiveness." And finally, when the time is right, tell him, "Jesus, I forgive and surrender this to you." Mother Mary will help you as well by interceding for you before her son, by praying with you for your natural mom, and by keeping her hands on your shoulders as you move ahead. If you do this, one day you, too, will find yourself sobbing with relief, hope, and joy.

CONCLUSION

This is why her love is as strong as death which no one can resist, which destroys every power and spares no age or rank. No sacrifice is therefore too great for her love, no trouble too burdensome. There is no obstacle to which she surrenders. So that she can carry out her task, she is allowed to see us in God as if looking in a mirror—us and all our needs and cares down to the smallest detail. Thus one can say she is omnipresent through her knowledge of us and through her unlimited love for us.[41]

—FR. JOSEPH KENTENICH

My sister flew in a couple of days before my mother's memorial Mass. On one of those days, we drove up to the retirement home where Mom had lived in order to look through her belongings. We had been given permission by the attorney to do so, and were grateful for his invitation. Granted, there were plenty of bad memories, but there were some good ones, too. Plus, our mother's life was entwined with our father's and our own lives. We wanted to see if there were any mementos of Dad or our childhood worth keeping.

Mom's room was left as it had been when she died, so going in gave me a cold feeling in the pit of my stomach. We were never allowed into my mother's side of the bedroom she shared with Dad, and after his death, I was never allowed into the room she had by herself. It was as if she would suddenly appear in the doorway, and my sister and I would be in big trouble. The two of us stood there, not really knowing what to do at first. Thank goodness my sister is organized and task-oriented; otherwise, I would have been lost. Once she started going through Mom's things, I was able to loosen up and help her.

There was not much at all. On the wall were a couple of pictures from my brother's visit with his family many years before. He had framed them for her. There was a copy of my oldest son's baby picture. On my visits, Mom was always so sure it was a picture of one of us kids. I knew she was wrong but never corrected her; it did not seem worth the trouble in her phase of dementia. There was a robe, slippers, and a few items of clothing in the closet and some underwear and pajamas in the dresser. The nightstand drawers were filled with odds and ends—batteries, a flashlight, costume jewelry, candy (Mom had a real sweet tooth in her elder years), and miscellaneous papers. Her rosary was there and a box with some personal items in it including her work ID and a couple of pictures of her on the job as a parking lot attendant. But there was not one picture of Dad or any of us kids. Her wedding ring was nowhere to be found. Her radio was still atop the nightstand next to where her head was when she slept.

It felt like we were sorting the property of a deceased stranger—snooping into some unknown person's private life. It was awkward. We gathered the rosary, pictures, and other things we wanted to keep, a handful, really. I was glad to see that Mom had hung on to the set of teakwood carvings that had been a gift of Jungle Jim. Jungle Jim (his nickname) was a kindhearted young man who had become friends with Dad and Mom through a citizen action group when I was very small. He traveled with the power company, laying cables across the ocean floor, and his job took him on exciting adventures to exotic places. He had had a special place in his heart for me, a sickly child who had stirred his compassion. He wrote me dozens and dozens of long, fascinating letters about his travels. They were always written on one of those amazingly thin, self-sealing blue air mail sheets, and he'd write very small so he could fit a lot in. I loved those letters and sometimes would take them to school to share with my class. The letters have long since disappeared—I do not know what happened to them. We took the carvings down from the wall, and I brought them home to remind me that there were some truly beautiful things about my childhood.

As we were leaving Mom's room, my sister abruptly stopped next to the dresser and looked down. Then she started to cry. I came up next to her and saw what she had spotted. It was one of those giant chocolate bars with a post-it note stuck on it. On the little, yellow square was written, "This belongs to Eva Steinhage."

"That's just so sad," my sister said, tearfully. "I can't believe it. She did not have much of anything. That's all that's left."

We left the chocolate bar right where we had found it and walked out.

Mom's life was filled with misery, and in her misery, she made others miserable. Her life was over, and it made me sad to think that so much of it had been spent struggling and bearing the consequences and burdens of her abused childhood. I do not believe that any mother actually wants to be abusive; I think they are all products of their upbringing and environment. There are people who have argued vehemently with me about this. I hear what they are saying, but I still disagree. I think that deep down inside, all mothers want to be good mothers out of instinct if not resolve. It just does not always develop that way. Some mothers who have been abused or mistreated as children are stronger, more receptive to God's grace, and can turn themselves around. Some, like my mother, try, do a bit better, fail, try again, and fail again. Many are resistant to God's grace and its power to transform. For some, the abuse does not just harden the character and spirit but causes mental illness. It seems that is what happened to my mother, and I accept that even though I do not like it one single bit.

Acceptance, peace, forgiveness, and closure—that is really what it is all about and what I have tried to guide you through in this book. I have shared a good deal more with you than I have shared with anyone, but I felt it was necessary so that you would understand that I do indeed understand because I have lived it. It can be extremely hard to accept what has happened to you in your childhood and how you have been treated by your mother. I think the tendency is either to point angry fingers and seek justification or look away and pretend that it never happened at all. It did happen. You must accept that it happened, and you must work through it, preferably with the help of a spiritual director and perhaps also a professional counselor. In working through it, you need to find peace and reach the point of forgiveness. That requires a lot of patience, prayer, and persistence. Finally, there will be closure. I personally do not think you can simply decide to have closure. Rather, I think that closure comes to you—God decides and provides the means by which you eventually can let go of the past, live in the present, and look to the future with hope and confidence.

There are two keys to attaining this: trust in God and love of Mary. The heavenly Father in his divine wisdom knows what is best for you, even when you feel as though all is lost. You have not suffered for naught—there is a reason, and good will come of it. The Holy Spirit nourishes your soul and inspires you so that you can be strong and courageous in the toughest of situations. Our Lord Jesus Christ is the ultimate healer; he will mend your wounds and restore you to health and vibrancy. Mother Mary will nurture and protect you. In her tender, loving way, she will accompany you each step of the way. She is, and wants to be in every way possible, truly your mother. What your natural mother did not give you, Mary has in store for you and is anxious to fill the void that has been left in you. She hears—has heard and will hear—your cries of distress, and she anxiously waits to answer them.

I am absolutely certain that Mary's love and protection are what kept me safe and helped me heal from the consequences of my mother's mental illness. Working beside her son and in unison with the blessed Trinity, my Blessed Mother saw to it that I would not only recover from my childhood, but would go on to help others recover from theirs as well by pointing the way to her. Do you know what the best part of all this is? The best part is that Mary is not just my mother; she is your mother, too. What Fr. Kentenich said in the quote at the beginning of this chapter about Mary's motherly love for her children is absolutely true. She loves you with a love that is as strong and death. No burden is too heavy for her, no sacrifice too great, and she will allow nothing to get in the way of her love for you! She sees and cares about you down to the smallest detail of your life. You are her special child and God's special child, and she knows that he has an important mission for you—one that no one can carry out but you. If that were not the case, you would not be here right now reading this book!

My prayer for you is that you will be able to grasp the mission that is given to you and that one day you will look back on your past with understanding and gratitude. Depending on where you are at presently in your relationship with your mother, I pray, through Mary's intercession, that someday you will be able to say with a sincere heart, "I forgive you, Mom, and I love you."

Sound impossible? It is not.

At the end of my mother's memorial Mass, I knelt in the pew preparing to say my thanksgiving for the beautiful celebration of the Eucharist—something I do at the end of every single Mass I attend. The music had gone still, and the guests were starting to file out. I knelt in the first row, with the life-size crucifix hanging before me. I looked at our Lord in his agony and knew he understood all that I had experienced growing up with my mother. On the right side of the altar was a picture of the Blessed Mother holding her son—the Mother Admirable, Queen and Victress of Schoenstatt. I repeated her Schoenstatt title silently in my mind, "Mother Thrice Admirable, Queen and Victress." She had always been my mother, even when I did not pay much attention to her and did not fully accept and respond to her love. She had always been the queen of my heart, reigning over me at all times, even when I ignored her. And she'd become my victress, fighting for me in the spiritual, emotional, and mental battle with my natural mother. She fought for me and she won.

I looked once again at the crucifix, gazing at the wounds on Jesus's hands, feet, and side. I intended to thank him for the privilege of receiving him in Communion. Instead, the words that sprang from my heart were these: "I forgive you, Mom, and I love you."

PART TWO

NOVENA

INTRODUCTION

I have said many times throughout *Forgiving Mother* that healing from the wounds caused by a troubled mother or difficult mother-child relationship takes time, patience, and prayer. Whether you navigate the process on your own, with a spiritual director, a professional counselor, or both, it cannot be done without God's grace. When we pray, we call upon that grace, opening our hearts to it and allowing it to penetrate our entire being. And so it is fitting that prayer frames this book, and for this I have chosen what I call a Marian Novena of Healing and Peace.

In case you are not familiar with novenas, let me explain. The word *novena* means "nine." A novena is a Catholic devotion that involves offering special prayers or services (like holy Mass, for instance) for nine consecutive days for a specific intention. This beautiful tradition hails back to Apostolic times when the apostles and Mary gathered in the Upper Room for nine days—from Jesus's Ascension to the coming of the Holy Spirit at Pentecost. They waited, prayed, and wondered what would come next. That was the world's first novena, giving rise to the practice of praying novenas to particular saints or for particular needs, seasons, or intentions, and it spread throughout the world.

Each day of the novena corresponds to one of the nine main chapters of the book, addressing the concerns and difficulties mentioned in the chapter and praying through them. As you probably noticed, the chapters build on one another. The book must be read front to back in order to follow the process and be fully beneficial. The novena follows the exact same course. You may want to pray a day of the novena at the end of the matching chapter. Or you may want to wait until you have read the whole book and then pray the novena. You might even wish to do both—pray along with the chapters and then again after you have finished the book. It is entirely up to you. The most important thing is that you open yourself to God's grace and Mary's love and do what works for you. We are all unique; what works for one person may not work at all for someone else.

Regardless of how you pray the novena, I hope that you do pray it. I do not know God's plan for you, nor how you will respond to it. You may receive answers to your petitions and feel at peace after praying the novena just once. You may need to pray it more than once, perhaps many times. You may pray it now and feel the need to go back and pray it again at some point in the future. Listen to how God is calling you and in what way your heavenly mother is touching your heart.

Above all, be assured that God hears your prayers, Mary feels and accompanies you in your struggle, and that I am praying with you. As I have worked on *Forgiving Mother*, I have prayed and offered sacrifices for every single person who will ever read this book and pray this novena. My prayers will not stop!

Lord, Give Me the Grace
to Want to Heal

Jesus asked the sick man at the Sheep Gate whether he wanted to be made well. That seems like an odd question, doesn't it? What person would not want to be well from an illness? On the surface, it seems obvious that the man had not already been cured because no one would put him into the pool when the water was stirred up. Still, our Lord questions his desire for a cure. He asks, not for his own sake, but for the sake of the sick man. He was looking for a testimony of faith from him. It was important for Jesus to know that the man trusted him, trusted his ability to heal him.

We can be very sick—suffering terribly—and still not want to be made well. This seems to be a recurrent theme in the healing narratives of the Gospels. There were many people who came or were brought to Jesus who were sick, crippled, or tormented and seeking to be well. Each time and in various forms, Jesus asks, "Do you really want to be well? Do you trust me to heal you?"

Until now, there was no one to put you into the pool. How long have you been waiting? Thirty-eight years, like the man at Bethesda? Or longer? Whether it is because you denied your woundedness or because you feared to share about it with anyone, you have stood alone in your suffering. You no longer need to stand alone. You no longer need to wait for someone to put you into the pool because Jesus is here, wanting to make you well and waiting for you to open yourself to his healing power.

MEDITATE

Read the following passage; then take a few minutes to let it sink into your mind and heart.

> They brought the boy to him. And when he saw him, the spirit immediately threw the boy into convulsions. As he fell to the ground, he began to roll around and foam at the mouth. Then he questioned his father, "How long has this been happening to him?" He replied, "Since childhood. It has often thrown him into fire and into water to kill him. But if you can do anything, have compassion on us and help us." Jesus said to him, "'If you can!' Everything is possible to one who has faith." Then the boy's father cried out, "I do believe, help my unbelief!" Jesus, on seeing a crowd rapidly gathering, rebuked the unclean spirit and said to it, "Mute and deaf spirit, I command you: come out of him and never enter him again!" Shouting and throwing the boy into convulsions, it came out. He became like a corpse, which caused many to say, "He is dead!" But Jesus took him by the hand, raised him, and he stood up. (Mark 9:20–27, NABRE)

REFLECT

Are you like the possessed boy's father? In many ways, you are like the parent of a tormented child. The difference is that this child is inside of you, part of you, and you do not know how to deal with him. Therefore, you do not want to deal with him because it is easier to pretend the torment is not there than to accept and face it. The prospect of healing is overwhelming, and you do not know where or how to begin. You can't bring yourself to do what it takes to heal the child, so you let him run free, grinding his teeth, foaming at the mouth, and throwing himself down like the boy in Mark's Gospel. The only way to end the torment is to bring the child to our Lord.

It is time now to stop avoiding healing, to stop being afraid to be made well, and allow Jesus to heal you. This first day of the novena is the beginning of a new life for you, a transformation in Christ. Yes, Jesus can and will heal you. But you must believe that he can heal you and trust in him.

ASK

Ask yourself the following questions. You may want to consider them while sitting in a prayerful place and speaking directly to our Lord. Or you may want to write your responses in a journal of healing and peace.

How have I been affected by my mother's mistreatment?

What has kept me from seeking healing until now?

Do I truly want to heal?

If not, why not?

PRAY

Jesus,

I am like the sick man lying next to the pool of Bethesda. I need healing but have no one to put me into the pool when it is stirred up. I want to be well, but am afraid of the process, and I am afraid to be put into the pool. I am afraid of what I will discover about myself and even more afraid of what I will discover about my mother and my relationship with her. Like the father with the tormented child, I feel as though it is easier to just leave him alone and let him run loose than to deal with him. I would prefer to pretend that my mother's mistreatment of me never happened.

Lord, it is so difficult to turn myself over to you and to trust in your ability to heal me. My unbelief is stopping me from reaching out to you, from allowing you to make me well. Please, help my unbelief.

Please, dear Jesus, grant me the grace to want to heal. Amen.

Finish this day's novena by praying the rosary for the grace to want to heal. Resolve to remind yourself three times during the day that you must trust in Jesus to be made well.

Mary, Let Me Grow Closer to You

While hanging on the cross, Jesus said to his Mother, "Woman, behold your son." And to John, his beloved disciple, he said, "Son, behold your Mother" (John 19:26–27, NABRE). This was more than a son's dying request to secure the care of his mother after he was gone. It was our Lord's plea for Mary to in fact become the mother of St. John and for St. John to in fact become her son. Furthermore, it was Jesus's request for Mary to be Mother to all human beings for all time. Despite his extreme suffering, Jesus did not issue this request out of desperation, but rather he spoke it with great feeling and purpose. He intended to give his Mother to us so that she could become his instrument in caring for us.

Our Lord knows your suffering, and he spoke those words just for you. It is hard to imagine, but he saw you from the cross. He saw you, he saw your natural mother, and he saw the way she has treated you. And so he gave you another mother, a spiritual, heavenly mother who would love, nurture, and intercede for you.

Meditate
Read the following passage, then take a few minutes to let it sink into your mind and heart.

> When Jesus had crossed again [in the boat] to the other side,
> a large crowd gathered around him, and he stayed close to

the sea. One of the synagogue officials, named Jairus, came forward. Seeing him he fell at his feet and pleaded earnestly with him, saying, "My daughter is at the point of death. Please, come lay your hands on her—that she may get well and live." He went off with him, and a large crowd followed him and pressed upon him.

While he was still speaking, people from the synagogue official's house arrived and said, "Your daughter has died; why trouble the teacher any longer?" Disregarding the message that was reported, Jesus said to the synagogue official, "Do not be afraid; just have faith." He did not allow anyone to accompany him inside except Peter, James, and John, the brother of James. When they arrived at the house of the synagogue official, he caught sight of a commotion, people weeping and wailing loudly. So he went in and said to them, "Why this commotion and weeping? The child is not dead but asleep." And they ridiculed him. Then he put them all out. He took along the child's father and mother and those who were with him and entered the room where the child was. He took the child by the hand and said to her, "*Talitha koum*," which means, "Little girl, I say to you, arise!" The girl, a child of twelve, arose immediately and walked around. [At that] they were utterly astounded. He gave strict orders that no one should know this and said that she should be given something to eat. (Mark 5:22–24, 35–43, NABRE)

REFLECT

In many ways, Mary is like the synagogue official, Jairus. The official's daughter is dying, and he runs to Jesus, interceding for her life. He believes that Jesus can heal his daughter. Because of the way you have been treated by your natural mother, you may feel as though you are dying, as well—dying a sad, painful death on the inside. Your heavenly mother, Mary, does not want you to die. On the contrary, she wants you to live a full, blessed life, so she intercedes for you before her Son. "My child is at the point of death. Please, come lay your hands on her—that she may get well and live," Mary tells him. Jesus responds, "Do not be afraid; just have faith."

Jesus will bring you back to life, not only because his mother has asked for this on your behalf, but also because he loves you. He wants you to be unafraid and to have faith in him. He also wants you to allow Mary to be your mother just as he requested of St. John as he stood at the foot of the cross. He knows that becoming a child of his mother is the surest way to heal from the wounds caused by your natural mother. It will take time and patience, but it will happen if you open your heart to her right now.

ASK

Ask yourself the following questions. You may want to consider them while sitting in a prayerful place and speaking directly to our Lord. Or, you may want to write your responses in a journal of healing and peace.

How do I feel about Mary?

What is my relationship with her?

What obstacles do I face in deepening my relationship with her?

How can I begin to remove those obstacles?

PRAY

Dear Mary,

My relationship with my natural mother has made it difficult for me to draw close to you. It is sometimes hard for me to trust you and to feel comfortable in your love, yet I know that this is what I need to be healed from the wounds I bear. I want to be like the beloved disciple, St. John, and take you into my home, into my heart, and to care for you and to allow you to care for me. That is asking a lot of me right now, and I need your intercession and God's grace to do it.

Mary, will you help me? Will you draw close to me even if I step away from you? Will you love me even if my heart cannot yet respond to your love?

Mary, please reveal yourself to me as a true mother. Please pray for me to have faith in your Son to heal me and trust in you to mother me. Amen.

Finish this day's novena by praying the rosary for the grace to want to draw close to Mary and allow her to be your mother. Resolve to recall three times during the day Jesus's words from the cross, "Behold, your mother."

DAY THREE

MARY, HELP ME LOOK BACK

Looking back on the past can be absolutely terrifying. When memories arise, you might want to dispel them rather than accept them. You may experience sudden flashbacks or you may find yourself reliving parts of your childhood because something in the present triggered your memories and emotions. That can be troublesome, especially if it takes you by surprise. Certainly, you do not want to live in the past, but on the other hand, you do not want to run from it either. Looking back can be very, very scary and yet it does not have to be so. It is okay to look back—even necessary—and can be enlightening and fruitful when you allow our Lord to open your eyes and help you to see. As your vision becomes less clouded, take Mary's hand and ask her to accompany you so that you will not stumble.

God has a plan for your life. He did not plan for your mother to mistreat you—she chose that on her own free will, likely as result of her own woundedness—but he has taken into account what your mother had done. He knows what has happened to you, and he knows how to use it to mold you into the person he has always intended for you to become. He has a way of making all things work for good, and that includes the abuse you have endured. But before you can become who you are meant to be, you need to look back at who you were.

Read the following passage, then take a few minutes to let it sink into your mind and heart.

> They came to Jericho. And as he was leaving Jericho with his disciples and a sizable crowd, Bartimaeus, a blind man, the son of Timaeus, sat by the roadside begging. On hearing that it was Jesus of Nazareth, he began to cry out and say, "Jesus, son of David, have pity on me." And many rebuked him, telling him to be silent. But he kept calling out all the more, "Son of David, have pity on me." Jesus stopped and said, "Call him." So they called the blind man, saying to him, "Take courage; get up, he is calling you." He threw aside his cloak, sprang up, and came to Jesus. Jesus said to him in reply, "What do you want me to do for you?" The blind man replied to him, "Master, I want to see." Jesus told him, "Go your way; your faith has saved you." Immediately he received his sight and followed him on the way. (Mark 10:46–52, NABRE)

REFLECT

Bartimaeus was blind physically, but he represents people who need more than just healing of their bodies. He represents those of us who need spiritual, mental, and emotional healing as well. Believe it or not, he represents you. You may not realize that you need healing, or you may be afraid to ask because healing involves change, change that could cause pain. So, like the blind man, you sit by the side of the road, trapped in your darkness and begging for help. But the kind of help you want and the kind of help you need in actuality can be two very different things.

The healing process means looking back on your past, and in that regard, you may wish to remain blind. Looking back means facing the reality of how your mother treated you and the impact it's had on you. No one wants to relive pain—sometimes it seems better to try to forget about it or ignore that it's there. Instead, you might prefer to just stay where you are.

Jesus nearly passed by Bartimaeus, but he isn't passing by you. He's here with you, now, next to you, waiting to heal you. He won't force his healing on you; rather, he's waiting for you to call out to him, "Jesus, son of David, have pity on me." What's more, Mary is here as well. She's like the Apostles who beckoned the blind man to come forward so that Jesus could cure him. She's beckoning to you now, and is eager to walk with you toward her Son so that you can be healed.

ASK

Ask yourself the following questions. You may want to consider them while sitting in a prayerful place and speaking directly to our Lord. Or, you may want to write your responses in a journal of healing and peace.

What is it in my past that I prefer not to see?

What do I think might happen if I look back?

How do I handle traumatic memories?

Whose help might I seek to better handle them?

PRAY

Dear Jesus and Mary,

Like Bartimaeus, I am stuck by the roadside, begging. In my blindness, I cannot help myself, and admittedly, sometimes I do not want to help myself. I do not want to look back on the past because I do not want to face the traumatic memories. I am afraid of what I might see if I look back. And so I remain blind, preferring that others do for me what I know I need to do for myself. In my blindness, I am helpless and at times even hopeless. Only you, Lord, can make me see again. Jesus, Son of David, have pity on me.

Mary, I am learning how to love and trust you. Please, reach out to me. Take my hand and lead me to your Son so that he can heal my blindness and mend my woundedness. Stay with me and guide me as I begin to see and to look into the past. Stay beside me and let me feel your motherly love for me.

Jesus, please have pity on me. Heal my blindness and give me the strength and courage to look back at the past and accept it as part of God's plan for me. Bless my relationship with your mother so that it will grow deeper and more secure. Amen.

Finish this day's novena by praying the rosary for the healing of your blindness and the strength and courage to look into the past with Mary as your companion. Resolve to ask for the healing of your blindness three times during the day.

Mary, Let Me See Myself as a Child of God

You may not be able to see yourself as a child of God right now, but in time you will. If you have been raised in the Catholic faith, you likely have been taught—either by one or both of your parents or a catechism teacher—that you are a child of God. Those are words that have a tough time sinking in when you are the daughter or son of a troubled mother. To hear and know that you are a child of God is not the same as feeling as though you are. Perhaps you have been neglected or demeaned by your mother. Maybe you have been beaten or otherwise abused. Or it could be that you and your mom are estranged because you just do not see eye to eye. Regardless, if you never sensed that your mother believes in you, it is difficult to believe in yourself.

Mary believes in you. She believes in you, and she loves you more than you can imagine. You are special to her, and for that reason, she is always by your side whether you are aware of it or not. She knows the joy of being a child of God and she wants you to experience that same joy. Mary wants you to feel as though you are a child of God, loved and cherished by him as though you are the apple of his eye.

Meditate

Read the following passages, then take a few minutes to let them sink into your mind and heart.

At that time the disciple approached Jesus and said, "Who is the greatest in the kingdom of heaven?" He called a child over, placed it in their midst, and said, "Amen, I say to you, unless you turn and become like children you will not enter the kingdom of heaven. Whoever humbles himself like this child is the greatest in the kingdom of heaven. And whoever receives one child such as this in my name receives me. Whoever causes one of these little ones who believe in me to sin, it would be better for him to have a great millstone hung around his neck and to be drowned in the depths of the sea. (Matthew 18:1–6, NABRE)

And people were bringing children to him that he might touch them, but the disciples rebuked them. When Jesus saw this he became indignant and said to them, "Let the children come to me; do not prevent them, for the kingdom of God belongs to such as these. Amen, I say to you, whoever does not accept the kingdom of God like a child will not enter it." Then he embraced them and blessed them, placing his hands on them. (Mark 10:13–16, NABRE)

REFLECT

Jesus speaks plainly. When he says that children are valued and important, he means that children are valued and important. To demonstrate this, he took a child to himself and told his disciples, "Whoever humbles himself like this child is the greatest in the kingdom of heaven." A second time, Jesus did similarly, telling them, "Let the children come to me; do not prevent them, for the kingdom of God belongs to such as these." There is much symbolism in Jesus's actions. In the first passage, Jesus asks a child to come to him. In the second passage, he did not just ask for the children to come to him, but he became "indignant" because the disciples were trying to stop them! Jesus points to the child as an example for all his followers because he knows that children love in simplicity and entirety. Children are accepting, trusting, guileless, and uncomplicated. The kingdom belongs to those who can love the heavenly Father with a pure heart.

Becoming childlike is the key to becoming free of the turmoil and misery of your past. Jesus is asking you to come to him, and if anyone tries to stop you, he will become indignant at them. He loves you and knows your value. He wants you to know your value as well. What has been said or done to you does not matter—nothing can change the fact that you are God's child. Once you become convinced of that, you will be able to look at your past, live in the present, and anticipate the future in confidence.

Turning to Mary will help you. She loves you and believes in you in ways your natural mother could not and may never be able to. Like her son, Mary wants you to come to her and to rest in her arms so that she can hold you close and whisper in your ear the many, many marvelous things that make you a person of great value. She wants you to believe in yourself and to truly feel as though you are a child of God.

Ask

Ask yourself the following questions. You may want to consider them while sitting in a prayerful place and speaking directly to our Lord. Or you may want to write your responses in a journal of healing and peace.

Do I believe in myself? If not, why not?

What parts of me don't I believe in?

What has made me feel that way?

What qualities do I have that are valuable and lovable?

PRAY

Mary,

Your Son drew the children to him because he loved them and knew how valuable they were. He wanted his followers to understand that value and to imitate their childlikeness so that they would be welcomed into God's kingdom. There is a message for me in our Lord's actions—a message I have not heard before but am hearing now.

Mary, you know what lies deep within my heart and you know how I feel about myself. You know how I have struggled and the things I need to work on so that I can truly feel as though I am a child of God. Please, take me by the hand and lead me through this process. It is hard for me to value myself, and I am depending on you to show me the way. You are my mother, and yet it is still hard for me to accept that and embrace you. Please, embrace me first and draw me to you. Please be patient with me, Mother Mary, in your gentle, motherly way, as my heart grows in love for you. Amen.

Finish this day's novena by praying the rosary for the grace to believe and feel that you are indeed a child of God. Resolve to ask Mary three times today to pray for you to grow in love for her and in security as a child of God.

MARY, LET ME SEE MY MOTHER AS A CHILD OF GOD

God created every single human being with a purpose designed specifically for him or her. Each person is his beloved child. That means that your mother is God's beloved child and has a specific purpose given to her by God. He alone knows what that is, and you can only trust that there is a purpose for her. Because he is the all-powerful, all-knowing, and almighty God, he is incapable of doing anything by accident. He intentionally created your mother, and he loves her as his own child because of that.

God gave us all something more besides life; he gave us free will, meaning that we have the privilege of choosing how we will act and respond to God's commandments. You have free will, and your mother has free will, too. Obviously, she has chosen to use it in ways that have been hurtful and perhaps even dangerous. That is not what God wanted for her or for you, but she chose to do it that way. On the other hand, God is also a God of justice, and your mother will someday have to answer, if she has not already, for the way she has treated you. And you will have to answer for the way you have treated her back.

MEDITATE

Read the following passage, then take a few minutes to let it sink into your mind and heart.

He was teaching in a synagogue on the sabbath. And a woman was there who for eighteen years had been crippled by a spirit; she was bent over, completely incapable of standing erect. When Jesus saw her, he called to her and said, "Woman, you are set free of your infirmity." He laid his hands on her, and she at once stood up straight and glorified God. But the leader of the synagogue, indignant that Jesus had cured on the sabbath, said to the crowd in reply, "There are six days when work should be done. Come on those days to be cured, not on the sabbath day." The Lord said to him in reply, "Hypocrites! Does not each one of you on the sabbath untie his ox or his ass from the manger and lead it out for watering? This daughter of Abraham, whom Satan has bound for eighteen years now, ought she not to have been set free on the sabbath day from this bondage?" When he said this, all his adversaries were humiliated; and the whole crowd rejoiced at all the splendid deeds done by him. (Luke 13:10–17, NABRE)

REFLECT

It must have been awful to be the woman who had suffered as a cripple for eighteen years, always bent over and never able to stand up straight. The Gospel does not say what it was that had crippled her, but one could speculate that it's some form of rheumatoid arthritis—a very painful and progressive disease. She was bent as if carrying a cross as Jesus had done up the hill of Calvary. Perhaps she was carrying a cross of some kind, put there by the burden of her own sins and woundedness. We do not know what causes her to be bent over; we only know that she was unable to stand erect and that Jesus, in his compassion, cured her.

Your mother is like the crippled woman. Her back is bent over, and she cannot straighten up. She might suffer real physical maladies, but she also suffers emotional and spiritual ones that keep her bent over. She suffers under the weight of her own sins and woundedness. You may not know what the weight is composed of, but you can tell that it is there because of the way she has treated you. Who knows how long she has carried that burden? Who knows how heavy it is for her?

It's time to spiritually lead your mother to Jesus, helping her through prayer to move her crippled body closer to him so that he can take the burden from her back and heal her, allowing her to once again stand upright. It is time to surrender your mom to God and let him take charge of her. Only he knows how to cure her crippled form. It is also time for you to surrender yourself with all of the pain, fear, and distress that you have suffered, carrying the heavy burden on your back all these years. Let go of your mom and all the anguish she has caused you and turn to Mother Mary. Allow her to take hold of you and accompany you further down the path to healing your own crippling and eventually to peace.

Ask

Ask yourself the following questions. You may want to consider them while sitting in a prayerful place and speaking directly to our Lord. Or you may want to write your responses in a journal of healing and peace.

What keeps my mother crippled and bent over?

What are the crosses she bears?

How has her past contributed to her abusiveness?

What good qualities does my mother have?

Pray

Dear Mother Mary,

My mother is like the arthritic woman in the Gospel who could never stand up straight. Like her, my mother has suffered for many years. Her suffering, her woundedness, has caused me to suffer as well. You know what has caused the crippling in my mother even if I do not. You know the burden she bears even though I cannot see it. You also know what it will take for her to be cured. Please, Mother, intercede for her before your son and ask him to heal her so that she can be the child of God that she was meant to be.

I surrender my mother now to you, Mary, placing her into your care and into the charge of Jesus. Please give me the grace I need to see my mom as truly a child of God and to really believe that she is. Then, I surrender to you myself and all that I have suffered, turning to you as my heavenly mother. Amen.

Finish this day's novena by praying the rosary for the grace to believe and feel that your mother is indeed a child of God. Resolve to mentally, emotionally, and spiritually surrender your mother to God three times today.

Mary, Let Me Be Transformed in the Spirit

It can be unbearable to even think that you could possibly have anything in common with your mother. With all that she's done and the way she's behaved, you probably want to be as much unlike her as you can be. Given the fact that you were born from her womb, you share the same genes, and some similarity is inevitable. Even if you were adopted or fostered, the mother who raised you passed on some of her traits merely because you shared the same environment and lifestyle.

However, you must remember that each of you was created by a loving God and for a specific purpose and that each of you is a child of God. Sharing characteristics with your mom is not always a bad thing. It can actually be a good thing when you share positive traits and when the bad or mediocre ones have been either eradicated or transformed.

Meditate

Read the following passage, then take a few minutes to let it sink into your mind and heart.

> Moving on from there, he went into their synagogue. And behold, there was a man there who had a withered hand. They questioned him, "Is it lawful to cure on the sabbath?" so that they might accuse him. He said to them, "Which one

of you who has a sheep that falls into a pit on the sabbath will not take hold of it and lift it out? How much more valuable a person is than a sheep. So it is lawful to do good on the sabbath." Then he said to the man, "Stretch out your hand." He stretched it out, and it was restored as sound as the other. But the Pharisees went out and took counsel against him to put him to death. When Jesus realized this, he withdrew from that place. Many [people] followed him, and he cured them all, but he warned them not to make him known. This was to fulfill what had been spoken through Isaiah the prophet:

"Behold, my servant whom I have chosen,

my beloved in whom I delight;

I shall place my spirit upon him,

and he will proclaim justice to the Gentiles.

He will not contend or cry out,

nor will anyone hear his voice in the streets.

A bruised reed he will not break,

a smoldering wick he will not quench,

until he brings justice to victory.

And in his name the Gentiles will hope." (Matthew 12:9–21, NABRE)

REFLECT

The man stretched out his withered hand, and Jesus restored it so that it became a healthy hand. United with the Spirit, Jesus transformed the man's hand into something brand-new. When the Pharisees ridiculed him for unlawfully curing someone on the Sabbath, Jesus pointed out that if one of their sheep fell into a pit on the Sabbath, he would grab onto it and lift it out in order to save its life. Human beings are far more valuable than sheep, Jesus said.

It is as if your heart is withered like the man's hand. It has been withered by the mistreatment and loneliness you have faced. Perhaps you feel as though you will never be emotionally, mentally, or spiritually healthy again. But, you are more valuable than any sheep; you are precious in the eyes of God, and he will heal you no matter where you are or what day it is. Like the man's withered hand, Jesus wants to transform your entire being into a strong, healthy being in body, mind, and spirit. He will pull you from the pit and save your life. He wants to use his grace to perfect your nature.

The prophet Isaiah wrote that God would place his Spirit upon his servant, that he would bring justice to victory and give hope to all people. Jesus is here now to bring your justice to victory and to give you hope. He is waiting to transform you in the Spirit so that your withered heart will be restored to health.

Mary observed as Jesus ministered to the people (Matthew 12:46, NABRE). She convinced him to perform his first miracle at the wedding in Cana (John 2:1–11, NABRE). It does not say directly in Scripture, but perhaps she was present when Jesus healed the man's withered hand. She knows her Son's power to heal and she wants him to heal you; she wants you to be completely transformed in the Spirit so that your heart is no longer withered but fully alive and fervent.

Ask

Ask yourself the following questions. You may want to consider them while sitting in a prayerful place and speaking directly to our Lord. Or you may want to write your responses in a journal of healing and peace.

What is my reaction when someone tells me I am like my mother?

Why do I react that way?

How am I like my mother?

How am I unlike her?

PRAY

Mary, my mother,

I struggle with the idea of being like my natural mother. I do not want to be like her in any kind of way, but I cannot help it. No matter how hard I try, I will always share some of her characteristics and traits. That frightens me. It can sometimes even make me angry at myself. It is a horrible predicament.

Jesus healed the man with the withered hand because he was so precious to him. I am precious to Jesus, too, and my heart has been withered by the strain of abuse and loneliness. I need to be transformed in the Spirit. I need my nature and all the things I have in common with my mother to be perfected by God's grace. I need to see that there is goodness in the qualities I have and learn to love and appreciate myself just the way I am.

Mother, pray for me. Invoke the Spirit to transform me into the healthy, grace-filled person God wants me to be. Amen.

Finish this day's novena by praying the rosary for the gift of transformation in the Spirit. Resolve to stop three times during the day to pray, "Come Holy Spirit, come."

Mary, Draw Me into Your Heart

You have a home in Mary's heart, and she is waiting for you to come home. Like all good mothers, she knows your voice and recognizes it among all the voices of all the people in all the world—even if all of them were talking at the very same time! When Mary hears your call, she will come rushing to your side to tend, mend, and protect you. You are her child, and she loves you with all her heart.

When the Little Flower was gravely ill, she and her family prayed to the Blessed Mother for a cure. It seems nothing would make the child well again. Then, one day as Thérèse's sisters were praying around her bed, she looked up at the statue of Mary that rested on her dresser. The statue smiled at her, and at that moment, Thérèse was made well again. Mary had drawn the little girl into her motherly heart and interceded for a miraculous cure.

Meditate

Read the following passage, then take a few minutes to let it sink into your mind and heart.

> When he entered Capernaum, a centurion approached him and appealed to him, saying, "Lord, my servant is lying at home paralyzed, suffering dreadfully." He said to him, "I will come and cure him." The centurion said in reply, "Lord, I am not worthy to have you enter under my roof; only say the

word and my servant will be healed. For I too am a person subject to authority, with soldiers subject to me. And I say to one, 'Go,' and he goes; and to another, 'Come here,' and he comes; and to my slave, 'Do this,' and he does it." When Jesus heard this, he was amazed and said to those following him, "Amen, I say to you, in no one in Israel have I found such faith. I say to you, many will come from the east and the west, and will recline with Abraham, Isaac, and Jacob at the banquet in the kingdom of heaven, but the children of the kingdom will be driven out into the outer darkness, where there will be wailing and grinding of teeth." And Jesus said to the centurion, "You may go; as you have believed, let it be done for you." And at that very hour [his] servant was healed. (Matthew 8:5–13, NABRE)

REFLECT

The centurion asked Jesus to cure his paralyzed servant who was suffering at home. Because the centurion believed in Jesus's healing power, he felt unworthy for the Lord to go to his house to heal the servant. Rather, he trusted that Jesus could cure the servant from right where he was. The centurion, a man of authority himself, understood Jesus as a man of authority. He knew that if Jesus commanded it so, the servant would be made well. Jesus was amazed at the faith of this Roman commander and told his followers that there was no one else in Israel who had as much faith as he did. "You may go; as you have believed, let it be done for you," he said to the centurion.

Like the centurion, Mary has amazing faith. She accepted Gabriel's request to become the Mother of God even though she knew it was humanly impossible. "Behold, I am the handmaid of the Lord. May it be done to me according to your word," she said to the angel (Luke 1:38, NABRE). Mary had faith that God's Son would be conceived in her womb by the power of the Holy Spirit as Gabriel had promised.

It may seem to you that it is humanly impossible for you to be healed of the wounds caused by your mother. Humanly speaking, perhaps it is. But, as Gabriel assured Mary at the Annunciation, "For nothing will be impossible for God" (Luke 1:38, NABRE). No, nothing is impossible for God, and Mary knows that firsthand. Divinely speaking, it is perfectly possible for you to be healed.

Mary is asking you to have faith like the centurion's and her own—a faith born of trust and surrender. Mary's heart is filled with that faith, and she wants to share it with you. She is eager to draw you into her heart where she can provide you with the healing and peace of her Son. She has extended the invitation to you and is awaiting your approach. You need only step toward her.

ASK

Ask yourself the following questions. You may want to consider them while sitting in a prayerful place and speaking directly to our Lord. Or you may want to write your responses in a journal of healing and peace.

In what ways do I need mothering right now?

What have I not been given by my natural mother that I wish I had been given?

Am I able to ask Mary to give me what I lack? If not, why not?

How can I approach Mary to ask her for what I need?

PRAY

Dear Blessed Mother Mary,

There was a time when I was convinced that I was all alone in my suffering, that that no one could save me. I was wrong. I am not alone; you will accompany me, sheltering me in your heart. You can save me from whatever harm my mother can inflict, and you can rescue me from any danger that lurks. You can give me peace and protection.

I am stepping toward you now, Mother, and I pray that I will be able enter your loving heart without further hesitation. It has been a long road, but I have come this far and I am not turning back. I want to finish the journey with you.

Mary, please draw me into your heart. Amen.

Finish this day's novena by praying the rosary for the kind of faith that the centurion had. Resolve to pause three times during the day to spiritually enter Mary's heart and ask her, "Mother, draw me into your heart."

MARY, LET ME GROW

The process of healing is an organic one. Slowly, you grow from one living form into another, somewhat like the process in which a caterpillar grows from the larva stage, through the chrysalis, and finally into a butterfly. The butterfly does not form without God's grace and direction. Nor do you.

Good mothers nurture their children so that they can grow in an organic, godly way. Mary is your good mother, and she will see to it that you receive the nurturing you need to grow into the being God has planned for you. As in the wilderness, things often change and grow very slowly and sometimes quite rapidly. It will be that way with you also. But, the one thing of which you can be sure is that with your mother's nurturance, you will grow, and you will grow steadily.

MEDITATE

Read the following passage, then take a few minutes to let it sink into your mind and heart.

> When he came to the other side, to the territory of the Gadarenes, two demoniacs who were coming from the tombs met him. They were so savage that no one could travel by that road. They cried out, "What have you to do with us Son of God? Have you come here to torment us before the appointed time?" Some distance away a herd of many swine was feeding.

The demons pleaded with him, "If you drive us out, send us into the herd of swine." And he said to them, "Go then!" They came out and entered the swine, and the whole herd rushed down the steep bank into the sea where they drowned. The swineherds ran away, and when they came to the town they reported everything, including what had happened to the demoniacs. Thereupon the whole town came out to meet Jesus, and when they saw him they begged him to leave their district. (Matthew 8:28–34, NABRE)

Reflect

The demoniacs dwelled among the tombs that were in the hillside above the Sea of Galilee. Their savagery terrified the villagers, so no one would use the road along the tombs. They kept their distance because they knew how dangerous the demoniacs were. In their agony, the demoniacs sought out Jesus because they were afraid of him and yet at the same time submissive to him because he was God. His very presence tormented them. At their own request, Jesus commanded the demons to leave the man and enter into a herd of swine nearby, sending them running over the edge of a cliff. Even in his justice, Jesus has mercy.

This is not unlike the way you may have needed to manage your relationship with your mother. Like the demoniacs and the townspeople, your mother can be a danger to you in the sense that staying too close could harm yourself or your family. Perhaps you're only now sensing the danger and haven't yet distanced yourself. Either way you know which road you may not travel. But while the villagers avoided the road out of fear, you can avoid the road out of a conscious decision to do what is best for both you and your mom. Just as it's unhealthy for you to be the recipient of abuse, it's unhealthy for her to levy the abuse against you.

With Mother Mary to encourage and protect you, you know you have the ability to turn to Jesus and ask him to disperse the demons that haunt you and your mother. He has the power to remove all of the insults, attacks, humiliations, and infractions and relieve you of your suffering by commanding them to leave and sending them away, racing over the edge of the cliff.

Ask

Ask yourself the following questions. You may want to consider them while sitting in a prayerful place and speaking directly to our Lord. Or you may want to write your responses in a journal of healing and peace.

Is there something that makes me feel unsafe with my mother right now? Is it a real or perceived risk? If so, what is it?

Do I need to distance myself from her? In what way?

How will I know if and when it's time to resume contact?

Pray

Mother Mary,

The past has been very, very hard for me to withstand, and yet, without those experiences, I wouldn't be the person I am today. I want to grow from my experiences, and I know that you can nurture me so that I grow well and in the way that God intends for me. The growth will be slow and perhaps even painful at times, but as long as I have you by my side, I'll be able to persist.

My natural mother needs to grow, and you can nurture her as well. I place her into your care, Blessed Mother, and ask you to care for her in your tender, motherly way. Despite the hardships of the past, I want to see my mom as a child of God and give her the respect that she deserves. Please help me to do that.

Mother Mary, I ask you to nurture me so that I can continue to grow. Amen.

Finish this day's novena by praying the rosary for the grace to grow in a godly, organic way. Resolve to pause three times during the day to ask Mary, "Mother, please help me to grow."

Mary, Let Me Be Healed

Each day of the novena has led you further away from the tribulation of the past and closer to the healing and peace of the future. Much has been accomplished, and you have received many graces. God has enlightened your mind and touched your heart in ways you probably never expected. You have grown closer to Mary and have begun to see and feel her as your true mother.

Still, the process of healing is ongoing and often cyclical. Memories and emotions you have already processed will come back to you, but each time they come back, they will be easier to reprocess.

Meditate

Read the following passage, and then take a few minutes to let it sink into your mind and heart.

> When Jesus arrived, he found that Lazarus had already been in the tomb for four days. Now Bethany was near Jerusalem, only about two miles away. And many of the Jews had come to Martha and Mary to comfort them about their brother. When Martha heard that Jesus was coming, she went to meet him; but Mary sat at home. Martha said to Jesus, "Lord, if you had been here, my brother would not have died. [But] even now I know that whatever you ask of God, God will give you." Jesus said to her, "Your brother will rise." Martha said to

him, "I know he will rise, in the resurrection on the last day." Jesus told her, "I am the resurrection and the life; whoever believes in me, even if he dies, will live, and everyone who lives and believes in me will never die. Do you believe this?" She said to him, "Yes, Lord. I have come to believe that you are the Messiah, the Son of God, the one who is coming into the world."

When she had said this, she went and called her sister Mary secretly, saying, "The teacher is here and is asking for you." As soon as she heard this, she rose quickly and went to him. For Jesus had not yet come into the village, but was still where Martha had met him. So when the Jews who were with her in the house comforting her saw Mary get up quickly and go out, they followed her, presuming that she was going to the tomb to weep there. When Mary came to where Jesus was and saw him, she fell at his feet and said to him, "Lord, if you had been here, my brother would not have died." When Jesus saw her weeping and the Jews who had come with her weeping, he became perturbed and deeply troubled, and said, "Where have you laid him?" They said to him, "Sir, come and see." And Jesus wept. So the Jews said, "See how he loved him." But some of them said, "Could not the one who opened the eyes of the blind man have done something so that this man would not have died?"

So Jesus, perturbed again, came to the tomb. It was a cave, and a stone lay across it. Jesus said, "Take away the stone." Martha, the dead man's sister, said to him, "Lord, by now there will be a stench; he has been dead for four days." Jesus said to her, "Did I not tell you that if you believe you will see the glory of God?" So they took away the stone. And Jesus raised his eyes and said, "Father, I thank you for hearing me. I know that you always hear me; but because of the crowd here I have said this, that they may believe that you sent me." And when he had said this, he cried out in a loud voice, "Lazarus, come out!" The dead man came out, tied hand and foot with burial bands, and his face was wrapped in a cloth. So Jesus said to them, "Untie him and let him go." (John 17:1–44, NABRE)

REFLECT

Jesus wept when he saw that Lazarus had died. Not only did he weep, but John wrote that he was "perturbed and deeply troubled." Even though he was fully divine, he also was fully human and felt human sorrow just as we do. That means he understands the sorrow you've felt from your mother's abuse. Just as it grieved him to see Martha and Mary in such anguish over their brother's death, he is grieved by the anguish you've suffered over your past, and he's come to heal you.

In many ways, you've been in the tomb like Lazarus was. You've been closed off from the world, entombed in an abusive situation with a wounded, perhaps deadened heart. But now, Jesus has come to roll the stone away and to call to you, "Come out!" He wants to heal you and give you back to the world transformed by his grace. Mother Mary is at the tomb's entrance next to Jesus, with her arms open wide and waiting to enfold you in them.

Allow yourself the joy of picturing the two of them peering into the tomb, anxious to see you, to look into your eyes and to express their love for you. Let the past slip away and feel the love that they're giving you. Walk toward your mother and embrace her, secure in her protection. Jesus reaches for you and places his hands upon your head. He prays over you, looking up to his Father in heaven.

Then, he blesses you, and you know that you are finally healed and at peace.

Ask

Ask yourself the following questions. You may want to consider them while sitting in a prayerful place and speaking directly to our Lord. Or you may want to write your responses in a journal of healing and peace.

How might I still be dead inside?

What is the stone that keeps me in this tomb?

How will I feel when the stone is cast aside and I see Jesus and Mother Mary waiting for me at the entrance?

Pray

Dear Mother Mary,

There have been incredible hardships during this journey to healing and peace, and at the same time there have been incredible rewards. I know that there are more to come, but that the worst is over.

I entrust my natural mother to you and ask that you see to it that she is cared for and that she finds her way back to you and to your son.

I entrust myself to you and ask that you stay close to me always, drawing me deeper and deeper into your loving, motherly heart. Please help me to continue growing in my relationship with you truly as my mother.

Mother, pray for me to finally reach the healing and peace for which I've longed all this time. Please, let me be healed. Amen.

Finish the novena by praying the rosary for the grace of peace and healing, entrusting yourself to Mary as your mother. Resolve to pause three times during the day to tell Mary, "Mother, I entrust myself to you."

Acknowledgments

This book was a challenge from beginning to end, but well worth the frustration, anxiety, hard work, and even spiritual warfare that it cost me. I am convinced that this is the book I was born to write, and I am glad I did.

It would not have come to fruition without the incredible encouragement of my siblings or the love and support of my husband and children. My gratitude to editor and author Heidi Hess Saxton for helping me to get the ball rolling and to my Servant editor, Katie Carroll, for assisting me in balancing and refining the manuscript. My thanks also to all the wonderful people at Servant who have had a hand in making this book possible.

Additionally, I have to thank Fr. Joseph Kentenich for scooping me up and saving my life on the day he consecrated me to the Blessed Virgin Mary. His writings and example have taught me invaluable lessons and carried me throughout my life. So too, I give thanks for the amazing Schoenstatt Fathers and Sisters who took me under their wings as I grew and healed. I would have been lost without them.

Finally, I give thanks to Mary, the Mother Thrice Admirable, Queen and Victress of Schoenstatt for accepting me as her child and for loving and protecting me even in the darkest moments.

I am truly blessed.

1. "Devotion to the Blessed Virgin Mary," *New Advent*, 2012, http://www.newadvent.org/cathen/15459a.htm. Accessed November 18, 2016. Also see Luke 10:9–10.
2. Pope Paul VI, Apostolic Letter in the Form of Motu Proprio, *Credo of the People of God*, 30. Also see Luke 10:9–10.
3. Pope Paul VI, *Lumen Gentium*, 58.
4. Mary Pages, "The Apparitions of the Blessed Virgin Mary," http://www.marypages.com/. Accessed November 19, 2016.
5. Joseph Kentenich, *Mary, Our Mother and Educator: An Applied Mariology* (Waukesha, WI: Schoenstatt Sisters of Mary, 1987), 86.
6. Joseph Kentenich, *Free and Wholly Human—Collected Texts*, Herbert King, ed. (Germany: Patris Verlag, Vallendar-Schoenstatt, 1998), 215.
7. Joseph Kentenich, *Free and Wholly Human—Collected Texts*, vol. 2, Hubert King, ed. (Germany: Patris Verlag, Vallendar-Schoenstatt, 1998), 24.
8. Pope St. John Paul II, General Audience, July 26, 2000.
9. Not to be confused with the Buddhist practice of mindfulness.
10. St. John of the Cross, "The Ascent of Mount Carmel," *The Collected Works of St. John of the Cross*, (Washington, DC: ICS, 1979), book 2, chapter 3.
11. St. John of the Cross, book 7.
12. St. John of the Cross, book 4, chapter 1.
13. Susan Muto, *John of the Cross for Today: The Ascent* (Notre Dame, IN: Ave Maria, 1991), 128.
14. St. John of the Cross, book 3, chapters 2, 9.
15. Kentenich, *Mary, Our Mother and Educator,* 170.
16. International Theological Commission, *Memory and Reconciliation: The Church and the Faults of the Past*, http://www.vatican.va/roman_curia/congregations/cfaith/cti_documents/rc_con_cfaith_doc

_20000307_memory-reconc-itc_en.html. Accessed November 23, 2016.

17. Francis W. Johnson, ed., *The Voice of the Saints: Counsels from the Saints to Bring Comfort and Guidance in Daily Living* (London: Burns and Oates, 2015), 108.

18. Joseph Kentenich, *God My Father* (Waukesha, WI: Schoenstatt Sisters of Mary, 1977), 74.

19. Joseph Kentenich, *God My Father,* 56.

20. Joseph Kentenich, *God My Father,* 58.

21. St. Theodore the Studite, Catechesis 32.

22. St. Thomas Villanova, quoted in John Baptist Pagani, *Anima Divota* (n.p.: R. & T. Washbourne, 1916), 163.

23. Thomas Aquinas, *Summa Theologica*, part 1, question 1, article 8.

24. Jeanne Heiberg, "The Rosary: Meditating on the Mysteries of Faith," *Catechist*, http://www.catechist.com/articles_view.php?article_id=2719.

25. St. Louise Marie Grignion de Montfort, "History of the Rosary," The Holy Rosary, http://www.theholyrosary.org/rosaryhistory.

26. Blessed Pope Pius IX, Apostolic Constitution *Ineffabilis Deus* (1854), as quoted in *Manual for Marian Devotion, The Dominican Sisters of Mary, Mother of the Eucharist,* (Charlotte, NC: Tan, 2016), 84.

27. "Zélie Martin—A Mother's Heart," Readings, EWTN.com, https://www.ewtn.com/therese/readings/readng7.htm.

28. St. Thérèse of Lisieux, *Story of a Soul: The Autobiography of St. Therese of Lisieux*, 3rd ed., (Washington, DC: ICS, 1996), 34.

29. St. Thérèse of Lisieux, 60.

30. St. Thérèse of Lisieux, 66.

31. Pope Paul VI, *Lumen Gentium*, 11.

32. *Lumen Gentium*, 40.

33. St. Alphonsus Liguori, *The Glories of Mary*, Rev. Eugene Grimm, ed. (New York: Redemptorist Fathers, 1931), 53.

34. Carol Kelly Gangi, *365 Days with the Saints: A Year of Wisdom from the Saints* (New York: Wellfleet, 2015), 94.

35. Fr. Jonathan Niehaus, *Brushstrokes of a Father*, vol. 1: *The Storms of Youth* (Waukesha, WI: Schoenstatt Fathers, 2009), 19–21.

36. Niehaus, 53–54.

37. The Schoenstatt Covenant of Love is a consecration similar to that taught by St. Louis de Montfort. The Schoenstatt consecration, however, is interactive and includes a mutual exchange of hearts, goods, and interests. The focus of the Covenant of Love is the Schoenstatt Marian Shrine, where the Blessed Virgin is enthroned as Mother Thrice Admirable, Queen and Victress of Schoenstatt. There are more than two hundred such shrines and thousands of Schoenstatt members around the world.

38. Niehaus, 44.

39. Niehaus, 143–145.

40. Maria Faustina Kowalska, *Diary: Divine Mercy in My Soul*, 3rd ed. (Stockbridge, MA: Marian, 2005), 175.

41. Kentenich, *Mary, Our Mother and Educator,* 86.

Marge Fenelon is a Catholic wife, mother, award-winning author and journalist, blogger, and speaker. She was awarded the 2015 Egan Journalism Fellowship, which recognizes exceptional journalists with demonstrated excellence in reporting for Catholic media. With the fellowship, she traveled to the Philippines to report on the recovery and reconstruction efforts in the aftermath of Super Typhoon Haiyan. That same year, she was accepted to the Jordan Tourism Board Religious Journalist and Blogger Tour, traveling to Jordan to report on Jordan's unique character and historic biblical sites. In 2014, she was accepted to the Church Up Close Seminar for International Journalists hosted by the Pontifical University of the Holy Cross in Rome where she studied "Covering the Catholic Church in the Age of Francis." Also in 2014, she traveled to Israel with the Catholic Press Association as guests of the Israel Ministry of Tourism to experience and report on the Holy Land sites there. She's written for a variety of Catholic media including *National Catholic Register, Our Sunday Visitor,* CatholicMom.com, and *Catholic Digest.* She's a weekly contributor to Relevant Radio's "Morning Air Show" and is a popular guest on other Catholic radio and television shows. A popular speaker, she's known nationally for her warm, personal style. She's written several books about Marian devotion and Catholic spirituality. Her book, *Our Lady, Undoer of Knots: A Living Novena* received a 2016 Association of Catholic Publishers Award for Excellence in Publishing. Marge and her husband are consecrated members of the Apostolic Movement of Schoenstatt.

Printed in the United States
By Bookmasters